MISOGYNATION

Also by Laura Bates

Everyday Sexism

Girl Up

MISOGYNATION

THE TRUE SCALE OF SEXISM

LAURA BATES

**SIMON &
SCHUSTER**

London · New York · Sydney · Toronto · New Delhi

A CBS COMPANY

First published in Great Britain by Simon & Schuster UK Ltd, 2018
A CBS COMPANY

Essays first published in the *Guardian* newspaper between 2013 and 2017

1 3 5 7 9 10 8 6 4 2

Simon & Schuster UK Ltd
1st Floor
222 Gray's Inn Road
London WC1X 8HB

www.simonandschuster.co.uk
www.simonandschuster.com.au
www.simonandschuster.co.in

Simon & Schuster Australia, Sydney
Simon & Schuster India, New Delhi

A CIP catalogue record for this book
is available from the British Library

Hardback ISBN: 978-1-4711-6924-3
Trade Paperback ISBN: 978-1-4711-7414-8
eBook ISBN: 978-1-4711-6925-0

Typeset in Bembo by M Rules
Printed and bound by CPI Group (UK) Ltd, Croydon, CR0 4YY

Simon & Schuster UK Ltd are committed to sourcing paper
that is made from wood grown in sustainable forests and support the Forest
Stewardship Council, the leading international forest certification organisation.
Our books displaying the FSC logo are printed on FSC certified paper.

For all the unsung heroes,
with deepest gratitude.

Contents

CONTENTS

INTRODUCTION

This book is not a labour of love. In many ways, it would be more accurately described as a labour of frustration, or of anger. I am angry at the fact that women face an epidemic of sexual violence. I am frustrated by the routine discrimination they suffer in the workplace, and furious that almost a third of them are groped against their will before they even leave school. I hate the sexual harassment that pursues them in the street and on to public transport, the misogynistic way in which they are portrayed in the media and the gender stereotypes that force many of them into low-paid, part-time work with little chance of promotion. I am shocked that women still bear the vast burden of unpaid caring work, enabling the economy to flourish while going unnoticed and unrewarded. I'm outraged that 86 per cent of the cost of austerity has come from women's pockets, with vulnerable and poor women worst affected.

But perhaps most of all, it frustrates me that we fail to join the dots. We treat these and so many other problems as if they are entirely separate and unrelated issues. As if it is complete coincidence that a husband's murder of his wife, a man jailed for stalking and a woman whose hijab was ripped off in the street are reported on the front pages the very same day. We fail to see the pattern that is right in front of us and, in so doing, we fail its victims, over and over and over again.

When police warn women not to walk alone after a spate of assaults, when yet another new product pops up demanding women buy it to protect themselves from attack, when a politician is decried for having the audacity to complain about rape threats, all this is connected.

When we learn that women are dramatically under-represented in our parliament and businesses and then see our prime minister and the Scottish first minister on the front pages under the headline 'Never mind Brexit, who won Legs-it!', these things are related.

When a newspaper runs an article describing rape as a romp or a jury acquits an accused rapist because of the previous sexual history of the accuser, these are not isolated incidents.

When a black woman is asked where the toilets are by a male attendee of the conference she is due to speak at, when a woman in a wheelchair is physically pushed aside by a man in the street, when a trans woman is bullied in the workplace or an older woman is completely ignored by a shop assistant, these are interconnected, not separate issues.

Until we join the dots, we haven't any hope at all of stopping misogyny. We can't tackle any one of these incidents in isolation. We can't improve the representation of women on FTSE 100 boards or in our government without tackling the mindless, racist gender stereotyping that sets girls' sights lower and constrains their ambition before they even reach primary school. We can't resolve the scourge of domestic violence or female genital mutilation without also taking on the societal norms that see women routinely spoken about, and to, as if they are second-class citizens whose sexuality exists solely to satisfy and be policed by men. We can't address the enormous gap in pay between men and women, or between white women and women of colour, without recognizing the overt and unconscious bias that exists at every level of the job market.

Nor is any of this coincidental. It is deliberate, systematic and ingrained. It is built into the systems, the institutions and organizations that make up our society. It is revealed in the fact that our senior judiciary is overwhelmingly dominated by white men; that our criminal justice system remains institutionally saturated with prejudice; it is evident in the pitiful statistics that reveal women make up less than a quarter of professors at UK universities and that, at the time of writing, no black academics have worked in senior management in any British university for the past three years. That no woman has ever held the position of chancellor of the exchequer, BBC director-general or governor of the Bank of England. That in the five years leading up to 2015, just four black women appeared on the flagship BBC current affairs programme *Question Time*. That there is just one female editor of a major UK daily newspaper and over three-quarters of front-page articles are written by men.

What's more, the cycle of acceptance is perpetuated by the fact that women are groomed their whole lives to consider these experiences inevitable, and society is conditioned to see them as normal. It is consolidated by the silence of those who witness the behaviour of men like Harvey Weinstein (accused of sexually harassing, raping and assaulting dozens of women over decades) and choose to turn a blind eye, complicit in their silence. It is enabled by the culture of workplaces, from Westminster downwards, where sexual harassment is dismissed as 'high jinks' and women who dare to complain are branded troublemakers. And it is cemented by a media that responds to the first tentative allegations of such behaviour in decades with reports of a 'witch hunt' gone too far.

We are so often told that these are unrelated problems. 'Lone wolf'. 'Domestic affair'. 'Isolated incident'. These are the terms used to excuse and erase the crimes of middle-class white men. Yet to anybody paying any attention at all, day after day, week after week, the bigger picture is maddeningly apparent.

These columns grew out of frustration, out of a need to bear witness. To try, week after week, to say: 'Look! There, and there, and there again! See the pattern? See the similarities?' They grew out of a hope that perhaps, by documenting as many as possible of these incidents of the type that are so often instead ignored, there might be a chance of the bigger picture emerging. And they grew, too, out of a sense of awe and admiration of the women who fight on, tirelessly, in spite of everything, striving to join the dots and change the picture.

So this book is a labour of anger, yes, and of frustration. But perhaps it is a labour of hope as well.

MISOGYNATION

RIDICULOUS SEXIST
ARGUMENTS BUSTED

Being a feminist means listening to a lot of really stupid arguments. It simply comes with the territory. People's efforts to justify, excuse or deny sexism are so numerous that you can even divide them into different categories.

There are the self-defeating trolls: 'There's no such thing as sexism . . . you stupid bitch.'

The anti-feminists, who don't realize the answer is feminism: 'Why should I support women's rights when men still have to pick up the bill at dinner?' (Answer: because feminism fights for women to have the financial independence required to split the cheque.)

And then there's the downright ludicrous. I once genuinely encountered somebody who argued that women in Saudi Arabia were lucky not to be allowed to drive because it meant they were involved in fewer car accidents.

It's no coincidence that a lot of these arguments aren't logical. They don't spring from carefully considered reason, but from panic – a knee-jerk terror that feminists, in fighting for equality, must be hell-bent on taking something away from men. Each and every small feminist advance, from recording misogyny as a hate crime to putting the image of a woman on a banknote, is met with a backlash. The irony is that these responses, which allege hysteria and 'PC gone mad' are often far more hysterical and out of proportion than the developments they seek to criticize.

The widespread normalization of these arguments is what makes them so pernicious. We have all heard it said that women should take care walking alone at night, or that maternity leave puts an awful strain on businesses. These opinions are so frequently recycled that it is easy for them to become mistaken for facts. In an unequal society, much goes unchallenged because we are so used to hearing the ostensibly reasonable justifications that help to maintain the status quo. But when we begin to unpick some of these commonly recited mores we start to realize that the arguments we've accepted for so long are actually full of holes.

WOMEN SHOULD NOT ACCEPT STREET HARASSMENT AS 'JUST A COMPLIMENT'

Walking down a quiet street at around 7pm a few nights ago, I noticed, without thinking anything of it, that there were two men coming towards me in the opposite direction. It being dark but for the street lamps, it wasn't until they came quite a lot closer that I started to notice the telltale signs. As they neared, the men were overtly looking me up and down, eyes lingering on my breasts and legs, before turning back to one another, saying something I couldn't hear, and sniggering. My heartbeat quickened, the hair rose on my arms and I felt the usual emotions flood through me. Fear. Anxiety. Impotence. Anger. Frustration. Misplaced embarrassment and shame.

This is one of the things I think some men don't understand, the men who ask you what the big deal is about street harassment, say they'd love it if it happened to them, or suggest you just 'take it as a compliment'. It's not a simple, one-moment experience. It's a horribly drawn-out affair. The process of scanning the street as you walk; the constant alert tension; the moment of revelation and the sinking feeling as you realize what is about to happen. Countless women have written to me about the defence mechanisms they put in place – walking with keys between their knuckles just to feel safe – wearing their earphones so they can keep their head down and ignore it. The whole process of going out, particularly at night, can become fraught and difficult.

Why don't you just take it as a compliment?

Too late to cross the street, I braced myself for the moment of passing, muscles tensed, cold fists involuntarily clenched. I understand that this must sound like an overreaction. But it isn't. Because the way we think and behave is shaped by our previous experiences. Too many times, in my own experience, this situation has turned from leering to aggressive sexual advances, from polite rebuttal to angry shouts of 'slag', 'slut', 'whore'. Once, I was chased down the street. Once, I was trapped against a wall. Once, my crotch was grabbed suddenly, shockingly, in vitriolic entitlement. So yes, my muscles contracted and I drew into myself as they passed.

For a moment, they paused, and one glanced at my breasts before turning nonchalantly to the other. I was expecting the usual. 'Look at the tits on that' or 'I wouldn't say no'. But what he actually said took my breath away:

'I'd hold a knife to that.'

The other man laughed, and they walked away without giving me a second glance.

And that, in a nutshell, is why I don't take it as a compliment. Because it's not a compliment. It's a statement of power. It's a way of letting me know that a man has the right to my body, a right to discuss it, analyse it, appraise it, and let me or anybody else in the vicinity know his verdict, whether I like it or not. It's a power that is used to intimidate and dehumanize members of the LGBTQIA community, who suffer disproportionate levels of street harassment. It's a 'right' that extends even to the bodies of the 11- and 12-year-old girls who have written to the Everyday Sexism Project in their thousands, describing shouted comments about their breasts and developing bodies as they walk in their uniform to school. Street harassment is no more about compliments than rape is about sex. Both are about power, violence and control. That's why, when women have the temerity to reject the advances of street harassers, they so often turn, in a moment, to angry outbursts of abuse. Because that rejection disrupts their entitlement to our bodies, which society has allowed them to believe is their inherent right.

This doesn't mean the end of compliments. It doesn't mean you can't flirt, or be attracted to a stranger, or make a polite approach and strike up a conversation. Those are all completely different things from commentary about your body that is directed at you, not to you; the dehumanized discussion of your parts by a group of passers-by, not caring that you can hear, or a scream of 'sexy' or 'slut' or 'pussy'. Those aren't compliments. They're something else. I believe that the vast majority of people know the difference. If you're really not sure, err on the side of caution.

This is not to suggest that every woman is a cowering victim, or that we're all too scared to go about our business on a daily basis. Just that it would be nice if those people who think street harassment is 'just a compliment' recognized the very real and enormous impact it has on victims' lives – not just in the moment, but day in, day out. A compliment doesn't make you rethink your route the next time you walk down the street. Many women, including Doris Chen, who grabbed hold of a man on the underground after he ejaculated on her, have bravely confronted their harassers. But the point is that they shouldn't have to. Nobody knows how they will react in that situation until it happens. Often, victims report feeling frozen with shock. Sometimes it isn't safe to respond. Instead of telling victims how to react, we should focus on preventing it from happening in the first place. And we can start by debunking the myth that street harassment is just a bit of harmless fun.

Originally published 28 February 2014

TEN MYTHS THAT BLAME WOMEN FOR SEXISM

When you're a woman who spends a lot of time talking about sexism, you start to notice that about one in ten of all the replies you receive begins with the same two words: 'Yes, but ...' Whether you've just outlined economic disadvantage or structural oppression, described workplace discrimination or discussed harassment at school, there will always be somebody who tries to argue that, in fact, it's women themselves who are to blame for the problem. This 'yes, but' phenomenon happens so frequently that you start to recognize the same arguments being trotted out again and again; so often, in fact, that you start to wonder if it would be useful to have the responses to them all in one convenient place ...

1. 'Yes, but girls just aren't that interested in science'

Take a baby, bring it up in a world that screams at it from every angle that it should be interested in certain subjects and not in others. Then, at the age of fifteen or so, ask it what subjects it would like to study, and shriek excitedly that society was right all along – girls just aren't that into maths or science! QED.

2. 'Yes, but if a girl's wearing a short skirt, she's asking for it'

The first flaw in this argument is that it implies the parallel assumption that every man is an animal with such uncontrollable urges that he's unable to prevent himself assaulting a woman who is wearing a particular piece of clothing. The second is that it's not backed up by facts. Most victims are already known to their rapists, debunking the theory that it's a random act provoked by a piece of clothing. Support charity Rape Crisis explains: 'People, and especially women and girls, of all ages, classes, culture, ability, sexuality, race and faith are raped. The perceived "attractiveness" of a victim has very little to do with sexual violence. Rape is an act of violence, not sex.' Oh, and the third flaw? Women should have the right to wear whatever the hell they want without fearing assault. That's setting the bar pretty low.

3. 'Yes, but women go off and have babies – why should companies pay the price?'

It's amazing that this still needs addressing, but some people still see pregnancy as some sort of selfish little jaunt at an employer's expense. The argument goes that small businesses in particular can't be expected to suffer the financial consequences if a woman wilfully flounces off to procreate, leaving them in the lurch. The glaring omission in the argument, however, is that – contrary to popular belief – there tend to be men involved somewhere in the process as well. Women aren't gleefully knocking themselves up for a nine-month 'holiday' – they are continuing the human race. As such, it isn't unreasonable to expect society, including businesses and other workplaces, to share the financial cost. Where this is problematic for businesses, it's because we haven't yet sufficiently provided the necessary financial and organizational infrastructure to facilitate the process, not because greedy women are causing them trouble.

4. 'Yes, but it's women who buy and write the women's magazines you criticize'

This is a classic chicken-and-egg situation. We bring girls into an image-obsessed world, where they're taught from birth that their inherent value is mostly in their looks. We raise them in a society that bombards them with images of thin, blonde, long-legged, smooth-skinned, tanned, large-breasted women, and implies that these women are 'better' than the 99 per cent of human females who don't happen to look that way. Then we deride them for buying magazines that promise to teach them how to lose weight, smooth their skin and perfect their looks. If we changed the culture – the way we treat women, and the expectations they grow up with – we might find that media supply and demand would change, too.

5. 'Yes, but women make different life choices'

Usually used to counter evidence of gender imbalance in top business positions, the problem with this argument is that it stops there. The point shouldn't be that women 'choose' family over career, but that we still live in a society that forces them, in so many cases, to make that choice at all – while men are able to enjoy high-flying jobs and have children without sacrificing either. Yes, women may choose to have children, but they don't choose the structural set-up of a society in which few options (shared parental leave, flexible working hours, childcare) are widely available enough to allow them to do so without compromising their careers.

6. 'Yes, but women objectify men, too'

Two wrongs don't make a right. And there's a reason why the people who voice this argument nearly always cite the Diet Coke advert ... because there are far fewer memorable examples of male objectification to choose from. Yes, men are objectified, too, but not to such an extent, so frequently, or to the exclusion of their other attributes – as is the case for women. So it doesn't have the same wide-ranging negative impact on society's view and treatment of them. (Not to mention that two wrongs don't make a right ...)

7. 'Yes, but women are their own worst enemies'

This argument seems to hold that, because some women are mean to some other women, we shouldn't have the audacity to tackle structural oppression until we've sorted out our own individual differences. But saying we should all be treated equally regardless of sex is very different from saying everybody should be nice to each other. This is a classic attempt to deflect attention away from ingrained inequality and instead on to women themselves, and leans heavily on the sexist stereotype of 'catty', 'bitchy' women.

8. 'Yes, but women are bad role models'

Blah blah blah, Rihanna, blah blah, Miley Cyrus ... It's not a coincidence that so many female singers perform extremely sexualized routines or wear very little clothing. They're women operating in a world that lets their male peers sing fully clothed and tells them they'll only sell records if they flash the flesh. It's another example of blaming and shaming women, focusing on the symptom and ignoring the cause.

9. 'Yes, but women just don't make good bosses'

This one always makes me laugh. It's invariably based on the speaker's own experience of three or four female colleagues, from whose individual failings they extrapolate the unfitness of the 3.5 billion or so other women on the planet. We've all had bad bosses, but we'd never look at a disorganized male colleague and assume that every other man in the world would have the same managerial style. Why do the same for women?

10. 'Yes, but why didn't she leave?'

Probably the most pernicious of all, this argument is usually directed at victims of domestic violence. It's a variation on a theme, which also includes such gems as 'Why does she always go for bad boys?', 'Why did she provoke him?' and 'Why didn't she see it coming?' It shows a deep lack of understanding of the psychological components of domestic abuse and the control an abuser can exert, but, most of all, it betrays a stubborn refusal to focus on the perpetrator instead of the victim. The best answer is the simplest: 'Yes, but why did he do it?'

Originally published 7 August 2014

WHY IS TRAVELLING ALONE STILL CONSIDERED A RISKY, FRIVOLOUS PURSUIT FOR WOMEN?

Women around the world have spoken out about their experiences of travelling after two young Argentinian women, María Coni and Marina Menegazzo, were killed while backpacking in Ecuador. In the wake of their deaths, online commenters seemed to blame the women for what had happened, asking why they were 'travelling alone'.

But, as Paraguayan student Guadalupe Acosta pointed out in a Facebook post that has been shared more than 730,000 times, there is an enormous double standard in asking questions like this of female travellers. It's the equivalent of asking women who have been subjected to unwanted sexual attention or violence what they were wearing, instead of focusing on the wrongdoing of the male perpetrators.

In response to the furore, the phrase *#viajosola* (I travel alone) trended on Twitter, with more than 5,000 women using the hashtag to discuss their experiences. One woman poignantly wrote: 'Travelling is freedom. Freedom has no gender.' Another wrote: 'I want to ... travel alone without the fear I'll be punished for it.' Another said: 'For women to stop travelling alone would be admitting we are to blame and have to be careful, when it is the world that has to change.'

Many people also rightly pointed out the irony of criticizing the two women when they were, in fact, travelling together. To suggest that women shouldn't travel even with female friends takes victim-blaming a step further still – implying that women shouldn't stray from home at all without male chaperones.

The truth is, women do experience a large amount of harassment and abuse while travelling alone, but they also experience danger in their local communities. To suggest that any woman shouldn't travel alone is illogical when no country has successfully tackled, and stopped, gender inequality and sexual violence.

The tragic case of the two backpackers, 22-year-old Coni and 21-year-old Menegazzo, is by no means the first of its kind. When 33-year-old New Yorker Sarai Sierra was killed in Turkey during her first trip abroad, online commenters questioned her common sense and asked why she was travelling without a male companion.

But Sierra's case (the man convicted of murdering her said the attack began after she rebuffed his attempt to kiss her) was strikingly similar to that of Mary Spears, for instance, shot and killed in Detroit in 2014, having rebuffed a man's advances, and to that of another woman who had her throat slashed by a man in New York (but fortunately survived) after she turned down the offer of a date.

The exact same fate might just as easily have befallen Sierra at home, but it didn't protect her from judgements and criticisms of her decision to travel. In this sense, there is also an element of racist stereotyping in our readiness to condemn crimes against women that happen abroad as representative of wider violent attitudes towards women. Meanwhile, we fail to make the same generalizations about attacks that happen at home.

To put things in perspective, according to the Foreign and Commonwealth Office (FCO), in 2013–14 there were 106 reported rapes of British nationals abroad and 152 reported sexual assaults. 'An Overview of Sexual Offending in England and Wales', released by the Ministry of Justice, Home Office and Office for National Statistics in 2013, revealed that 85,000 women are raped in England and Wales every year, of whom around 15 per cent report the incident to police. In the same way that confining women to women-only carriages on trains doesn't solve the problem of harassment, but restricts women's movements while tacitly condoning perpetrator actions, the same could be said about telling women to solve the problem of harassment and violence by staying at home. It unfairly curtails women's freedom, and suggests that violence against them is simply inevitable.

Yet the restriction of women's solo travel remains a curiously acceptable form of victim-blaming. When Sierra was killed, for example, one headline read: 'American's death in Turkey puts focus on solo travel'. Compare this with a headline about the death of Harry Devert, a 32-year-old US citizen killed while travelling alone in Mexico: 'The untimely death of world traveller Harry Devert'. When Australian Lee Hudswell died after an accident while tubing down a river in Laos, the press reported: 'Fatal end to Lee's overseas adventure'.

Female travellers have long been subjected to restrictions and double standards, with their gender emphasized over their capability and strength. Female travellers are much more likely to be categorized into reductive stereotypes – such as the glamorous adventuress – than their male counterparts. Think H. G. Wells in *Warehouse 13*, sexy Lara Croft or the film portrayal of Adèle Blanc-Sec versus that of Tintin. When men travel in films, they are usually just travelling, but when women do, they are often running away from (or towards) a male romantic partner. (Compare *The Holiday, Wild, Under the Tuscan Sun, Eat Pray Love* to *The Motorcycle Diaries* or *Into the Wild*.) There are, of course, welcome exceptions (take a bow, *Dora the Explorer*).

Travel has historically been, and to an extent still is, seen as a natural, bold activity for men, and a risky or frivolous pursuit for women. And as with so many other forms of low-level sexism, the knock-on impact is enormous. At a local level, curtailment of travel can prevent women from accessing healthcare, visiting family or taking job opportunities. When we inhibit women's wider freedom, we also limit their ability to broaden their horizons and acquire valuable language skills. The impact on women's careers can be clearly seen in the responses to female journalists who experience assaults while reporting abroad and face not only immense victim-blaming but also the curtailment of foreign assignments as a result.

When CBS correspondent Lara Logan was assaulted in Cairo in 2011 while reporting on the uprising, for example, one Canadian newspaper ran an article entitled: 'Women with young kids shouldn't be in war zones'. The (male) writer asked: 'Should women journalists with small children at home be covering violent stories or putting themselves at risk? It's a form of self-indulgence and abdication of a higher responsibility to family.' Another commentator asked: 'Why did this attractive blonde female reporter wander into Tahrir Square last Friday? What was she thinking?'

All travellers should take safety precautions, regardless of age or sex. Nobody is suggesting that women shouldn't make the same sensible preparations as their male peers. But any attempt to constrain women's movements solely on the basis of gender not only feeds into the idea that violence against them is inevitable, instead of tackling it, but also ignores the very real threats they face at home.

Originally published 21 March 2016

TEN FREQUENT COMMENTS ON FEMINIST BLOGPOSTS – AND MY RESPONSES

Journalist Helen Lewis wrote in 2012 that 'the comments on any article about feminism justify feminism'. In my experience, she was right. But it's not just the outrageous threats, misogynistic abuse and so on that emphasize the importance of the movement. It's also the more subtle responses; the denials and challenges, often repeated over and over, that prove the points that feminist writers are making. In the interest of satisfying some of these heroically persistent critics, here are the answers to the ten most common 'below the line' responses I've received.

1. 'This is not specific to any gender'

I like to think of these commenters as sweetly naïve rather than deliberately obtuse. Because, of course, were they to look at just a smidgen of the statistical evidence (often cited in the articles beneath which they are commenting), they would realize that these issues – harassment, sexual abuse, workplace discrimination – are very gendered indeed.

2. 'Well done. You have identified a problem that has been identified a million times. Now what is your solution?'

I feel *awful* for foisting another article about sexism on this poor beleaguered reader. As tough as it is for him to keep reading about it though, he might want to stop to consider what it's like to live with it day in, day out. Sure, articles highlighting a problem aren't necessarily a solution in themselves. But when

I first started Everyday Sexism, I met the same response again and again: 'Sexism doesn't exist any more.' It's impossible to begin to tackle something without first raising awareness that the problem exists.

3. 'Why are you whining about this when there are more important things in the world?'

It's amazing how this criticism is so rarely levelled at football writers, say, or people writing light-hearted pieces about DIY or dog walking. Curiously, in fact, it's almost exclusively women who are policed with the shouts of 'It's worse elsewhere, so think yourself lucky'. The existence of rape and other forms of sexual violence don't invalidate the experiences of those who are discriminated against in the workplace or harassed in the street; nobody tells the police to stop investigating fraud until they've solved every murder. The presumption that women in the UK have nothing to complain about is simply false: 85,000 women are raped in the UK every year and over 400,000 sexually assaulted. An average of more than two women are killed by a current or former partner every week. And perhaps most importantly of all, this argument fails to see the links between these different forms of oppression and violence. If we aren't allowed to challenge the more 'minor' forms of harassment and discrimination, we set a precedent for the treatment of women as second-class citizens that has a direct impact on the more serious crimes.

4. 'I don't know if these people can ever be changed'

It's probably true that people who are sexist or commit acts of abuse are unlikely to be swayed by a *Guardian* blogpost.

Revelatory. But I've heard from a lot of men who say reading these articles has made them rethink sexist behaviour that they had previously considered to be harmless. And it's my belief that there's a critical mass of people out there who wouldn't dream of carrying out such abuse, but also aren't aware that it's going on. If we can engage them, and open their eyes to the problem, they will be more likely to take action and become part of the solution. Maybe a dad will read one of these articles and be alerted to the importance of talking to his sons about respect for women. Maybe a woman who has been groped will read one and realize that she has the right to report the incident to the police.

5. 'If any man tries to grope me, they'll get a foot slammed somewhere they really don't want it to be'

I understand the impulse to comment on an article about harassment or groping with suggested reactions, I really do. It's frustrating to read about people experiencing abuse and it's a natural human response to offer advice. But these comments utterly fail to recognize the emotional and physical impact of being accosted or assaulted. More importantly still, focusing on responses fails to put the blame squarely where it really belongs – with the perpetrator.

6. 'We can all say "Men should not do that in the first place" but this is the same as me leaving my car door open with keys in it and saying "People should not rob"'

No, it's not. First, there is no good way to avoid assault – 90 per cent of rapists are known to their victims, so those old chestnuts about not wearing short skirts or going out late at night are nonsense. Second, we have to tackle perpetrators, not tell victims how to behave. Third, if you leave your car door open and your car is stolen, you're not likely to be widely shamed, to encounter a justice system consequently predisposed against you and jurors who are inclined to sympathize with your attacker while stigmatizing you.

7. 'What about cleaning adverts portraying men as clueless idiots?' ... 'Does Laura Bates really believe no man has ever been propositioned or felt up at work?'

Nope. In fact, the Everyday Sexism Project accepts and publishes entries from men. Yes, there are isolated examples of adverts and media that make negative and sweeping generalizations about men. But most of the articles I write are about women and their experiences of gender inequality. Why? Women experience gender inequality vastly more frequently than men. The inequality women experience tends to be much more severe than that faced by men. And because of the structural, ingrained inequality in the society we live in (economically, professionally, socially), incidents of sexism experienced by women tend to have a much more far-reaching impact on their daily lives.

8. 'I don't know anyone in my office who behaves that way' ... 'I just can't believe that happens regularly' ... 'I've never worked anywhere where these attitudes would be tolerated'

It's not hugely surprising that many male commenters may not have witnessed sexism or discrimination first-hand. Harassers and abusers often take advantage of moments of isolation, whether in a deserted tube carriage or an empty office. The silencing of victims means that many never tell anybody about their experiences. This is a problem that disproportionately affects women, so of course men are less likely to have seen it happening, but that doesn't mean it doesn't exist. You can keep trying to suggest the problem isn't really there because you haven't seen it, but there's a pesky amount of evidence to the contrary. Wouldn't it be easier just to believe us?

9. 'I don't think demonizing all men is going to help'

It's amazing how quick some men (yes, #notALLmen, don't panic) can be to jump to the conclusion that any article describing the actions of a minority must somehow be attacking them. It's not. But by jumping in to shout that not all men are like those described, you are becoming part of the problem. It's this kind of defensive response that makes it so hard to speak out about sexism. One great way to make the point that 'not all men' are sexist is to get involved in taking a stand – you can start by not derailing articles about the problem.

10. 'This is just another example of the feminist conspiracy at *The Guardian*'

Busted.

Originally published 4 September 2014

WHY DO THE POLICE STILL TELL WOMEN THAT THEY SHOULD AVOID GETTING RAPED?

'Women warned after Gainsborough assault.' 'Police warn women walking alone after riverside incident.' 'Serial sex attacker strikes again as ninth victim is assaulted and police warn women to be on their guard.' 'Police issue warning to women not to walk or travel alone after woman grabbed in latest incident.' 'Fugitive rapist: women urged not to walk alone as chilling footage at Manchester airport released.' These headlines represent five cases in one month alone where UK police have reportedly warned women to adjust their routines or behaviour because of crime in a particular area.

Many people reading these articles would nod approvingly and suggest that this is simply a common-sense measure, given the risk. Of course the police are also doing all they can to catch the perpetrator in each case – they aren't suggesting women should take sole responsibility for dealing with the problem. And yet, how absurd it would seem if we were to apply similar logic to any other type of crime . . .

'Police warn motorists not to drive after speeding drivers cause crashes in local area.'

'Police warn residents not to have garden sheds made out of wood after spate of arson cases.'

The idea of advising women not to walk or travel alone in an area where there has been a sexual assault might seem straightforward at first glance, but not everybody has the luxury of a car. Many people are dependent on walking, whether for their whole journey or to the nearest bus stop. As simple as it might sound to suggest travelling with a friend or family member, the reality of women's daily lives means that it would be near-impossible for most to arrange this and keep to their own busy schedules.

Surely this is obvious. Nobody is really expecting women in Clapham to venture out only in groups of three, armed with rape alarms and baseball bats. So what is the impact of issuing such advice? It starts to suggest to the general public that, specifically in cases of sexual assault, victims should be taking responsibility for their own safety and, implicitly, may be partly to blame if they are attacked.

If you think this is an exaggeration, just look at the first sentence from one of the articles: 'Women are being asked to take more care while walking around alone at night after an incident involving a man who reportedly tried to grab a woman on a riverside path.' Imagine reading this sentence as a recent victim of assault, as you deliberate whether or not to report what happened last night when you hurried home from work on your own in the dark.

The way we approach and discuss these topics matters. It has a huge impact. The most recent British Attitudes Survey (BSA) revealed that more than one-third of the British public – from whom rape trial juries are drawn – insisted that sexual assault victims bear partial responsibility for their attack if they have been 'flirting heavily' beforehand, and more than one-quarter believed they are partially responsible if they are drunk. This kind of police advice can only compound such attitudes.

The notion of telling women to take responsibility for their own safety from sexual violence is as old as it is ridiculous;

from women-only train carriages (which suggest male violence is inevitable and so women's behaviour and freedom
must be altered and constrained to accommodate it), to police
campaigns suggesting it is a victim's job to try to avoid being
raped. It sends an insidious message, reinforcing attitudes
that blame victims and allow perpetrators (cast as a blurry,
inevitable evil rather than determined, deliberate criminals)
off the hook.

Perhaps most worryingly of all, these messages are coming
from the institutions that are supposed to be tackling criminals, not policing victim behaviour. The past week also saw
'banter' about rape between members of the public and the
official Merseyside police Twitter account; an exchange that
was retweeted nearly 1,000 times. It comes hot on the heels of
revelations about officers who left an abusive voicemail on the
phone of a woman who had reported domestic abuse, calling
her a 'fucking slag' and a 'bitch'.

Now look back at the recent figures revealing that more
than a quarter of all sexual offences (including rape) reported
to the police are not even recorded as crimes, and ask yourself
how important attitudes towards sexual violence victims are.

This is a desperate situation, and demands active measures
such as training at all levels to counteract rape myths and
victim-blaming attitudes among those on the frontline of law
enforcement. We know that only around 15 per cent of victims of sexual violence feel able to report to the police. Isn't it
time we started asking why?

Originally published 5 September 2015

Everyday and Insidious

Drip, drip, drip. It's not a single incident that makes gender inequality so harmful. In fact, individual incidents are often maddeningly difficult to protest, quick as people are to respond that you're overreacting, imagining things or making a fuss about nothing.

The easiest way sexism seeps into our collective consciousness is by starting before we are old enough to challenge it. Pre-school girls worry about the size and shape of their bodies. Babygros in pink and blue promise future princesses and potential presidents, strictly delineated by gender. Research shows that parents interrupt girls more often than boys and that boys are more likely to speak up in the classroom. When children are taught that girls are particularly bad at a certain subject or activity, their performance declines accordingly. So what impact does it have when we tell them boys are naturally good at science, or sell them T-shirts that say 'I'm too pretty to do maths'?

By subjecting girls to sexism, harassment and assault before they are old enough to question it, we ingrain in them the notion that they are second-class citizens and must simply accept this behaviour as part of life. When sexual assault

25

becomes a normal part of the school day, we send the clear message that it is a normal part of daily life too. By excusing and praising boys and blaming girls for everything from sexual harassment to dress code violations, we teach them that women's bodies are men's to use, and that the fault lies with victims, not perpetrators.

I recently spoke at an event about some of the issues facing teenage girls, including body image pressure, mental health problems, online abuse and more. Seeing a little girl of nine or ten in the audience with her mother, one of the organizers went to warn the lady about the nature of the talk, concerned that the content might be too mature for such a young child. The mother explained that she was fully aware of the topics, and had brought her daughter on purpose. At the end, the little girl came up and thanked me. She said the talk had been particularly useful, because she'd received her first unsolicited 'dick pic' a year ago and hadn't known how to respond. At another talk, a shy 14-year-old came up afterwards and told me, in a voice barely louder than a whisper, that over the past year she'd been pressured by ten different boys to send them nude pictures of herself. Most of them she barely knew.

These little girls go on to grow up in a world in which they rarely see themselves portrayed in the media (particularly if they're disabled, transgender or girls of colour). Their stories just aren't told by the Hollywood machine that churns out hundreds of hit movies each year but affords women only 28 per cent of speaking roles and sees them remove their clothes three times more frequently than their male co-stars.

As they attend college or university, young women are faced with sexual harassment and assault often so extreme that those outside the education system would find it difficult to believe. Yet our stubborn societal insistence that gender equality has already been achieved makes it incredibly difficult to speak out about the reality of misogyny on campus without being branded an oversensitive snowflake. Young women aren't clutching their pearls and looking for something to complain about, as some right-wing commentators would have you believe. They are battling a litany of abuse in pursuit of their education, a situation so severe that many I have spoken to have simply dropped out of higher education altogether.

In September 2017, three major pieces of research were published in the same week. The first, a government-funded study, revealed that a shocking one in four girls is depressed by age fourteen. The second, a survey of 2,000 young people by charity Girlguiding, found that 64 per cent of teenage girls have experienced sexual harassment in the last year alone. And the third, The Global Early Adolescent Study, polled people across fifteen countries, showing that children felt straightjacketed into rigid gender roles in early adolescence, as the world expanded for boys and closed in for girls. Amid widespread coverage, I never saw anybody suggest a possible connection between these three sets of devastating findings.

And as the world around us sends us clear messages about our value and place, it also provides us with a litany of small examples of sexism, often combined with other forms of prejudice, so regular and expected that we slowly become desensitized to the situation. Part of dismantling the invisibility of gender inequality is taking off the blinkers that blind us to these daily abuses, because we are so used to the situation that we no longer even notice them at all.

YOU CAN TRACE A LIFETIME OF GENDER INEQUALITY THROUGH EVERYDAY SEXISM

In early 2012, I was groped on a bus in London. I was vocal about it and made sure everyone around me heard what had happened. Every other passenger looked out of the window.

Among the 100,000 stories submitted to the Everyday Sexism Project, near-identical experiences emerge again and again. Stories of women being masturbated at in public spaces came in their thousands, from Spain to Turkey, Germany to India. Women in Japan, England and Israel were told not to bother with higher education as it was their sole destiny to become homemakers for their future husbands. A woman was grabbed between the legs in a souk in Morocco and another had her crotch groped in a nightclub in China. A woman in North Africa was demoted by her boss for refusing his requests for sex and an employee in Europe was sacked when she turned down her superior's offer of a threesome.

Experiences shared by men and boys, such as being ridiculed for asking for parental leave, or suffering homophobic bullying for trying to stand up to lad culture, revealed the damage gender stereotypes do, not just to women but to everybody.

The stories came from people aged eight to eighty, be they wearing hijabs or bikinis, about sexism on aeroplanes and trams, at home, work and school. You can trace an entire lifetime of gender inequality through the experiences women have shared through the project . . .

It starts young. At eleven or twelve you begin to experience harassment . . .

'I was twelve, walking home after school, when a white van full of builders drove past honking and doing sexual hand gestures and shaking their heads with their tongues out.'

When you make it to school, the sexism continues . . .

'I'm eleven and I've just started high school. I'm constantly told by my peers and even my best friend that women should really just stay in the kitchen and clean so that guys can have a decent meal when they get home from work. They also make jokes about me and my friends being sluts and whores because we have breasts.'

Even within your family or an intimate relationship you may not escape sexism and violence . . .

'I was raped by my father as a child. When I first told this to someone I felt comfortable with, my current boyfriend, he made a rape joke and said: "Well, you shouldn't have led him on."'

When you reach university, you are bombarded with harassment and even assault on and off campus . . .

'In the nine months I've been at university, I've been almost raped, thrown against a wall for refusing to make out with a guy, threatened ("I'm going to fucking kill you, bitch") for standing up to a man sexually harassing my friend and groped or touched without consent on about 75 per cent of nights out. I'm sick of this.'

You graduate to a pay gap, and a workplace rife with sexism and harassment . . .

'I was told by my boss and his boss that they prefer not to work with women. Many men used foul language deliberately to put me off working with them. I was paid less than male colleagues I managed.'

When you choose to start a family, you risk losing your job because of maternity discrimination . . .

'I was brought into a company based on close to a decade worth of experience in my field. I then brought on nearly ten other highly experienced individuals. I had several former clients who loved me and loved my work . . . I was fired for being pregnant.'

On your way to and from work, you pass through public spaces which can be unsafe . . .

'Guys have grabbed my butt while I was walking on the street minding my own business, my crotch too . . . I constantly hear guys making comments about me, I am beeped on the street and I am shouted at with what they might see as "compliments". The last time a guy harassed me he said: "I would tear apart your ass."'

You walk past billboards and buses and magazine stands conveying an artificial ideal to which you are constantly compared . . .

'I don't have the giant boobs all the girls on the fronts of the magazines have. I don't have the giant boobs and the perfectly toned ass that all the girls in the music videos have . . . I don't have a little nose or perfectly straight white teeth. I don't have a flawless, airbrushed complexion like every single woman on any of the multiple face cream/make-up/toiletries/whatever else adverts I see every day. I have small boobs, some cellulite on my thighs, a kinda big nose, slightly wonky teeth and some facial scars from a car accident a few years ago. And I feel ridiculous. I feel that because of all these things, I'm not worth anything as a human being.'

The sexism you face might combine with other forms of prejudice . . .

'I overheard someone ask my boyfriend: "What's f***ing a Paki like?"'

Yet while all this is happening, other people seem not to see it . . .

'A man masturbated across from me and the woman sitting next to me on a bus one time. And he was moaning and saying things to us. And neither one of us stopped it or knew how to stop it. The rest of the passengers ignored it.'

If you try to stand up, you risk being bullied or harassed further . . .

'Was called a prude for objecting to Porn Fridays, where female colleagues' faces were Photoshopped on to porn pictures.'

If you try to speak out, you risk being belittled at best, disbelieved or blamed at worst . . .

'When I was raped, people said I was asking for it, that I was a slut and I had led him on.'

And yet, in spite of all this, people are standing up in their droves. According to the testimonies sent to Everyday Sexism, one group of teenage boys challenged sexism at their school by going in wearing skirts to show solidarity with the girls. University students set up a new feminist society to protest sexual harassment on campus. An engineer who was sick of being asked to do other people's photocopying broke the printer at work to avoid the problem. A woman sick of cold-callers asking to speak to 'the man of the house' started putting them on to her 6-year-old son. An employee whose male colleague loudly accused her of being on her period when she disagreed with him replied: 'If I had to bleed to find you annoying, I'd be anaemic.' A woman who was called an 'opinionated lesbian cunt' responded: 'Thank you. I'm proud of being opinionated, lesbian, and having a cunt.'

Every one of us has a moment when prejudice or inequality crosses our path, and we have a choice to make. Will you take a stand, or will you be the person who looks out of the window?

Originally published 16 April 2016

WHY DON'T TV SHOWS AND NEWSPAPERS CATER TO HALF THEIR AUDIENCE – WOMEN?

There is a cartoon by the artist Grizelda Grizlingham that shows a group of men sitting around a boardroom table, with only one woman present. The caption reads: 'Well, you're the only one who thinks we're a sexist organization.' The woman's face is fixed in a grimace. I can't help but think the cartoon would be equally accurate if a third or even half of the people around the table were women. Because, as recent history has shown, often nothing short of a full-scale campaign is enough to get people to listen to the perspective of 'just the women'.

Such was the case in the recent example of comedian Dapper Laughs, whose portfolio includes extreme misogyny, real-life harassment of women and rape jokes. Yet until a 60,000-strong petition was launched, ITV was apparently quite happy to defend his show as 'firmly based on treating women with respect and speaking to them in the right way' and 'neither sexist nor degrading to women', according to a letter one viewer received after making a complaint.

Although the broadcaster did finally decide to axe the show after a public outcry, it first attempted to defend it again, with a spokesperson saying: 'Comedy is subjective and we appreciate the content of the show might not be to everyone's taste. We regret that any of our viewers were offended. However, as with all of our shows, the series content was carefully considered, compiled and deemed suitable for broadcast.' This only sends one message to the viewer: we seriously thought about this and went ahead anyway. If you're likely to be upset by misogynistic content, you're not the core audience ITV was planning for. You are not the default viewer.

The same uneasy feeling might also have been experienced by female students at the University of Liverpool, when the script of a sexist, rape joke-fuelled play intended to be performed as part of an annual concert emerged on social media: this wasn't written with you in mind.

These aren't the only recent incidents to send women the clear message that they just aren't the target audience. How did *The Independent* think its female readers would feel when confronted by Frank Warren's recent column, headlined: 'Call me an old git, but I just can't see that there's a place for women's boxing'? What about heterosexual *Sun*-reading female football fans coming across its offer of a date with a page 3 girl as a prize for participating in their fantasy league? ('We might even let you pick which one, so feel free to start your research now.') Its response to criticism (which included saying that the promotion was unlikely to offend the 93 per cent male target audience) was so transparent, it may as well have been phrased as 'Calm down, love – this isn't for you.'

It's not just newspapers and television where women can find themselves crammed into repetitive, stereotypical roles or omitted altogether – it's true across other media as well, from gaming to theatre. And the experience of feeling 'this wasn't created with me in mind' is not exclusive to women – it is shared, in fact, by anybody outside the usually heterosexual, white, cisgendered, middle-class, non-disabled, 'default' target audience. Whether it's the hyper-sexualization and exotification of black women (a classic case of the intersection of gender and race); the portrayal of disabled people as tragic or evil; the stereotyping of particular religions; or the appearance of gay or transgender characters only in storylines about sexuality or gender identity, as if these characteristics entirely define them. These stereotypes erase and invalidate people's real and complex experiences, but those who object are often accused of being ungrateful – 'You should be happy they included that character at all.'

Of course, the problem isn't straightforward. Even in cases when writers try to push back against formulaic norms, as in the creation of the nuanced female character Skyler White in *Breaking Bad*, stereotypical expectations and judgements are so deeply embedded in audiences that the reaction can be a massive backlash against the character and even the actor involved. Actress Anna Gunn described her shock at discovering online forums with thousands of members dedicated to despising the character, where apparent hatred of the fictional Skyler's strength and refusal to succumb to her husband's wishes spilled over into death threats targeting Gunn herself.

These issues really affect the way we experience and consume media and entertainment. A stereotypical representation or a lack of diversity can act as a slap in the face that shakes a viewer out of the fictional world with the sharp realization: 'Oh, this wasn't meant for me.' You're left with the option of either tuning out, or guiltily continuing, with the uncomfortable feeling of squashing down your beliefs and personal experience, as *The Onion* perfectly captured with its headline: 'Woman takes short half-hour break from being feminist to enjoy TV show'. And the lasting impact is likely to run even deeper – a 2012 US study published in the journal

Communications Research found that watching more television generally lowered children's self-esteem … with the notable exception of white boys.

Perhaps the greatest irony of all is that a lack of media diversity doesn't even make good business sense. A recent study of diversity in Hollywood found that shows with diverse casts make more money and net bigger audiences. Yet the argument that such programmes are 'niche' or not 'mainstream' persists. Women make up more than half of TV audiences and the older we are, the more we watch, so why are women, and particularly older women, so under-represented on screen?

While the end product is a problem, it often originates from the lack of representation within media and entertainment industries themselves. But the excuse that there just aren't enough capable candidates available wears pretty thin when you look at the stable of work showcased by blogs such as *Media Diversified*, the success of circus company Extraordinary Bodies (which features D/deaf, disabled and non-disabled artists working equally together) or the track record of Madani Younis, the artistic director of the Bush Theatre, who presided over a year in which half of all stage shows were written by black and minority ethnic playwrights and half the main stage directors were women. Where there's a will, there's a way.

Originally published 13 November 2014

YOUNG CHILDREN MUST BE PROTECTED FROM INGRAINED GENDER STEREOTYPES

Scrolling through my Twitter timeline this week, one particular tweet, with an image attached, immediately jumped out at me. A parent had shared a snapshot of her 6-year-old child's homework – a worksheet asking pupils to research a scientist or inventor. So far, so normal. But the question, in jaunty Comic Sans, read: 'Who was he? Who was the person you have chosen to look at? How old were they when they began inventing? Did they have a wife and family?'

The frustration of the parent, who appealed to other Twitter users for suggestions of female inventors, would be dismissed by many as an overreaction to a carelessly worded question. But she is far from alone. Parents share similar homework woes with the Everyday Sexism website and Twitter account with startling regularity.

One referenced their son's physics homework, which used examples of men pushing vans, lifting weights, climbing trees and shooting arrows. The sole female example was a woman pushing a pram. Another parent described an assignment where children were directed to use a particular biographical research website, only to find that, of the twenty-one historical personalities listed, just two were women. One person's son had even been asked to compare the qualities of a 'good wife' from biblical to modern times (with no similar exercise discussing the merits of husbands). Numerous questions involved men doing active, strong tasks such as driving or playing sport, while women cooked, cleaned or, in one particularly bizarre example, simply 'sat on a rug'.

To those who cry 'overreaction', a new study published this month by the US-based National Bureau of Economic Research suggests that gender bias at primary school may in fact have long-term implications for pupils. The study saw several groups of students take two exams, one marked blind by outside examiners, the other marked by teachers who knew the students' names and gender. In maths, girls outperformed boys on the anonymously marked exam, but boys outperformed girls when assessed by teachers who knew their names, suggesting that they may have overestimated the boys' abilities and underestimated the girls. Tracking the pupils to the end of high school, the researchers found that boys who were given encouragement as youngsters not only performed better later on, but were also more likely to take advanced courses involving maths, compared with girls who had been discouraged. They concluded: 'Teachers' over-assessment of boys in a specific subject has a positive and significant effect on boys' overall future achievements in that subject, while having a significant negative effect on girls.'

Of course, many teachers actively encourage girls into STEM (science, technology, engineering and mathematics) subjects. But gender stereotypes are not only passed on at school. They also proliferate in the advertising, television, books, magazines and conversations that children are exposed to from a young age. In the strictly segregated aisles of many toy stores, blue shelves mark off chemistry sets, dinosaurs and building tools as the domain of boys, while girls are left holding the (plastic) baby.

Each individual incident is easily dismissed as harmless.

And, of course, there's nothing wrong with an individual child choosing to identify with any of these roles. But it's the assumptions made for them that matter. Young children are not always equipped, as most adults are, with the critical tools to analyse and probe information – what is presented as fact is often absorbed without question. This might seem extreme, until, as I have, you visit a variety of primary school classrooms and start to realize just how many under-tens genuinely think that girls simply aren't allowed to be footballers or doctors or lawyers. Ask your nearest small friend about these matters – you may be unpleasantly surprised.

The silver lining is that change is happening. Several toy stores have abandoned gender segregation, partly thanks to the efforts of campaigns such as Pinkstinks and Let Toys Be Toys. The parent whose tweet first caught my eye later reported an excellent response and apology from the school. There is hope, too, in the reactions of children themselves. According to one Everyday Sexism Project entry, a girl who faced her first experience of street harassment aged eight, when a passing man told her the muffin she was eating would 'go straight to [her] hips', patiently drew on her biology knowledge to explain: 'No, it won't, it has to go to my stomach first.' One mother described how, asked to complete a drawing for homework showing 'Mummy in the kitchen', her 7-year-old son added his daddy to the picture, doing the washing up.

It's refreshing to see how ridiculous sexism can look through children's eyes. If we could only restrain ourselves from passing our own inherited assumptions on to them.

Originally published 23 February 2015

THE POCKET MONEY GAP – AND TEN OTHER WAYS GIRLS ARE TAUGHT THEY'RE WORTH LESS

A new study has revealed that the gender pay gap begins as early as childhood, with boys on average receiving 20 per cent more pocket money than girls. While the disparity, which amounts to £2.20 per week, might not seem calamitous, the message behind it matters.

When we treat our children differently from such a young age, we send them powerful indicators about their worth, their strengths and what will be expected of them in adulthood. Taken together, these influences can have a major impact. Here are ten other ways in which girls are taught to devalue themselves.

1. Clothes

It isn't an exaggeration to say that the problem starts at birth. A recent viral image of two Babygros hanging side by side in a shop revealed dramatically different messaging. 'I'm super' was emblazoned across the blue version, while its purple counterpart read: 'I hate my thighs.' As they grow into toddlerhood, boys' clothes tend to be more robust and functional, with pockets and sturdy fabrics, whereas girls' attire is more flimsy and designed with a focus on appearance, not activity.

2. Toys

From the soft bunnies and dollies thrust into little girls' arms to the robots and building sets more commonly offered to boys, we subtly teach girls that they are expected to be passive, pretty and nurturing, while boys are given the opportunity to explore and learn. Girls are presented with pastel perfume-making kits instead of engineering sets, and boys are also taught by gendered and heteronormative toys from a young age that they aren't expected to take part in domestic activities like cooking, cleaning and childcare.

3. Books

Despite recent fantastic campaigns to improve the diversity of children's literature, many early-years books still present readers with stories about a nice, white daddy who goes out to work while the nice, white mummy stays at home baking cakes and looks after the children. Of course, there's nothing wrong with such a storyline, but if it's the only one that children see over and over, it creates a sense of what's 'normal' or 'expected' before they have even begun to consider their own future life choices. Not to mention the rather less subtle impact of books for girls with titles like *How to Be Gorgeous*, with the boys' equivalent, *How to Be Clever*.

4. Television

Research from the Geena Davis Institute on Gender in Media, which analysed 275 American children's TV shows, revealed that just 30 per cent of characters and 20 per cent of narrators were female. So we subtly let children know that boys are the main event and girls are more often observers or window dressing. Even more important, the research demonstrated how content can send subtle messages to children about their future potential: only a quarter of employed characters in the show were female, normalizing the idea that men are expected to be the main breadwinners.

5. Advertising

A 2012 Munch Bunch advert showed a little girl tottering around in red high heels and jewellery and a little boy lifting a broom above his head with the slogan: 'Grown up like Mummy and strong like Daddy'. It was the perfect example of how advertising can direct children's aspirations and teach them how they should expect to be valued in later life.

6. Party themes

Even children's parties convey a clear message about the sort of roles we expect girls and boys to inhabit, with princess and fairy party bags abounding in the pink aisle, while more adventurous pirate and superhero themes suggest boys are active and in control.

7. Behaviour

The influences aren't all external: it is also common for parents and other adults to socialize children from a young age to submit to certain gender stereotypes. Boys are proudly described as 'boisterous', as if it's a badge of male honour, while girls are more likely to be shushed, told to be still and quiet, and scolded for getting clothes dirty.

8. Fancy dress

One story that always sticks in my mind is from a mother whose toddler daughter grabbed a toy stethoscope at a playgroup, prompting another parent to swoop in immediately and cry: 'Ooh, you're going to be a nurse!' Nursing is a brilliant career option, of course, but would the same reaction have been elicited by a 2-year-old boy? When children are given opportunities to mimic future career options, particularly with fancy dress, girls are routinely offered options like nurse or beautician costumes, while little boys choose between jobs such as policeman, fireman and doctor.

9. Compliments

How often do we praise little girls for being pretty, sweet or beautiful, and little boys for being smart, strong or clever? These might seem like benign and well-meaning words, but repeated over and over again they start to ingrain the notion that girls are judged on their appearance and beauty, while boys' action and intelligence matter more. Of course, the same is also true of insults – few little girls reach their teen years without hearing someone ridiculed at least once for doing something 'like a girl'.

10. Money management

An early gender pay gap wasn't the only finding to emerge from the research into children's pocket money. It also revealed that parents are less likely to allow girls control of their own finances. While boys are given regular payments, teaching them to manage their money, parents are more likely to hold on to girls' money until it is needed, or to buy items on their behalf. So children learn from childhood that men control the purse strings and women are less trusted with money and maths.

Of course, none of these issues alone is a disaster. No single parental choice or TV show is to blame for socializing children into stereotypical gender roles. Nor is anybody suggesting that the answer is to force girls to dress only in blue or to provide nothing but dolls to every boy. But taken together, the impact is very real. So giving our children the widest possible range of choices, doing away with unnecessary gender segregation in marketing and improving the diversity of kids' entertainment could have a much bigger impact on their futures than you might think.

Originally published 24 January 2017

LITTLE GIRLS DESERVE BETTER THAN TO BE TOLD TO MAKE THEMSELVES SEXY

This week we have seen a toy cleaning set marketed by Sports Direct with the label 'It's Girl Stuff!' A few days later, news emerged that Harrods was offering little girls the chance to be turned into Disney princesses for just £1,000 a pop (or £100 for the princess on a budget). Then an Everyday Sexism Twitter follower alerted me to a website offering 'girly' games from *Bratz Makeover* to *Hollywood Beauty Secrets*.

The Harrods Disney experience, complete with sparkly makeover and deluxe princess dress, is aimed at girls aged three to twelve and culminates in an oath where princesses vow, among other things, to be 'kind and gentle'. Perhaps not the best advice for future boardroom battles or climbing the steely managerial ladder but, of course, those aren't the sort of roles one would expect a princess to aspire to. Girls lucky enough to be treated to the full £1,000 royal experience come away with a case full of make-up too – just the thing for the under-twelves!

Meanwhile, over on the Friv website (which seems to be aimed at a similar age range, if games such as *Where's My Blankie?* and *Girl Fashion* are anything to go by), young gamers are treated to a veritable smörgåsbord of options. But look closer, and almost every game, from *Selena's Date Rush* to *Back to School Makeover*, involves exactly the same steps. Players are presented with a cartoonish waif with a head nearly triple the width of her waist and charged with using 'beauty products' to make her presentable, from clearing spots to plucking brows to applying make-up. Whether the goal is a hot date or the first day back at school, the message remains the same: conforming to beauty standards and slathering on products is the number one priority for girls everywhere.

Thanks to games such as *Dream Date Dress Up* ('You have a dream date today ... wow him with your cuteness'), it's pretty clear that making yourself beautiful to attract a boy is the ultimate goal. The instructions to *Selena's Date Rush* are simple: 'When Justin comes to pick her up in the morning, she just woke up with no make-up! Please help her complete her make-up before Justin finds out!' Because heaven forbid her boyfriend should realize she doesn't sleep in full slap.

Sadly, these themes are by no means isolated to a single website – they are everywhere, from the website for tween sensation Monster High to Nickelodeon's own site. The latter includes such gems as *iKissed Him First* ('Carly vs Sam in a battle for a boy'), *Big Time Crush Quiz* ('Find out which Big Time Rush guy is right for you!') and *Makeover Magic*. On the Monster High site you can meet characters including Clawdeen Wolf – a 'fierce fashionista' whose hobbies are 'shopping and flirting with boys' but whose time is tragically consumed with removing leg hair: 'Plucking and shaving is definitely a full-time job.' It would almost be funny if it didn't make you want to weep.

And it doesn't end there. Over on the website of TOPModel Magazine, another big hit with the tween age range, girls learn that 'Mascara alone is not enough! You need more to achieve a radiant look!' There are even tips to get rid of cellulite by 'pinching yourself with a twisting hand movement'. Because they might as well learn young that inflicting pain on oneself in the name of beauty is a woman's lot.

So to return to those who think that making a fuss about these things is an overreaction, it is only when you look at all of this stuff together that you start to realize the immense impact it might be having on young girls. Everywhere they turn they are bombarded with the idea that their looks are everything, that their place is in the home, that pleasing the male gaze is paramount and that they are riddled with imperfections that need to be 'fixed'. As if the constant bombardment of hyper-sexualized, airbrushed media images of women wasn't enough to get the message across.

And things are only getting worse. One mother told me: 'My 7-year-old daughter told me "Barbie is fat" when she compared it to her Monster High doll.' Another said her 5-year-old daughter had asked to be turned into a boy so she could go into space. A 15-year-old girl wrote to us to say that 'I always feel like if I don't look a certain way, if boys don't think I'm "sexy" or "hot", then I've failed and it doesn't even matter if I am a doctor or writer, I'll still feel like nothing . . .'

So that's the answer for those people who want to know why we're getting our knickers in a twist – why we're getting so worked up about this. Because as long as our little girls receive the message, everywhere they look, that hiding their 'imperfections' and making themselves sexy is the sum total of their value, we are failing them. Frankly they deserve better.

Originally published 10 January 2014

TEN THINGS FEMALE STUDENTS SHOULDN'T HAVE TO GO THROUGH AT UNIVERSITY

A string of headlines about misogynistic behaviour has become a depressingly recognizable sign that the new university year has begun. For many female students, those headlines represent the tip of the iceberg. Should young women really still have to brave this barrage of sexist 'banter' in the process of getting a degree?

1. Being openly treated as sexual prey

For female students starting at Emmanuel College, Cambridge this month, a depressing welcome awaited. Student newspaper *The Tab* reported on a leaked email encouraging members of an all-male drinking society to 'smash it (/the girls)'. A student at a different university reported to Everyday Sexism that they had overheard a student halls rep telling a fresher: 'I'm going to treat you like a dolphin, segregate you from the group until you give in to me.' Others from different universities report 'points systems' for games such as 'fuck a fresher', 'seal clubbing' or 'sharking' – where older male students win points for sleeping with first-year girls. (In some cases, extra points were reported for taking a girl's virginity or keeping their underwear as a trophy.) In many cases, these are the people supposed to be looking after freshers as they settle in.

2. Sexism from sports clubs

The term had barely started at the London School of Economics before the rugby team was disbanded for distributing a homophobic and misogynistic leaflet calling girls 'mingers', 'trollops' and 'slags' and describing female athletes as 'beast-like'. This came after a Durham University rugby club's 'It's not rape if ...' drinking game and Aberystwyth University's cricket team going out wearing shirts bearing slogans such as 'casual rape'.

3. Misogynistic chants

At the University of Nottingham, a video has emerged showing a crowd of first-year students singing a chant including the lines:

> *These are the girls that I love best,*
> *Many times I've sucked their breasts.*
> *Fuck her standing, fuck her lying,*
> *If she had wings I'd fuck her flying.*
> *Now she's dead, but not forgotten,*
> *Dig her up and fuck her rotten.*

It echoes last year's video of students at Stirling University chanting on a public bus about sexual assault and miscarriage.

This certainly isn't just a British problem – it follows the story of last year's 'frosh week' chant at St Mary's University in Canada, which included the words: 'Y is for your sister / O is for oh so tight / U is for underage / N is for no consent / G is for grab that ass.' And a fraternity from Yale University that hit the headlines for marching through campus chanting 'No means yes! Yes means anal!' this year announced plans to expand to UK universities.

4. Freshers' week sexism

One student present at the University of Nottingham event told *The Guardian*: 'I was angry because it was the first night of my university experience, which I'd been looking forward to for a long time. I was upset that I was already experiencing misogyny on my first night.' And it's not unusual for freshers' week to see a spike in sexist incidents – last year, a freshers' week event was advertised to students at Cardiff Metropolitan University using a poster bearing the words: 'I was raping a woman last night and she cried.'

5. Sexist initiations

Female students wanting to get involved in clubs and societies often find themselves pressured or coerced into highly sexualized and often degrading initiations, from simulating oral sex to giving lap dances or taking their clothes off.

6. Being photographed without consent

After the recent proliferation of online 'spotted' and 'confessions' pages dedicated to specific universities, female students can find themselves photographed unawares in the library or elsewhere on campus, with their pictures widely commented on and rated. Those who aren't photographed might be treated to the joy of comments such as:

'To the hot girl sitting opposite me on level 3, do you mind if I have a cheeky danger wank whilst looking at you?'

'To the sexy brunette on the 4th floor, will you be my girl-frien? I didn't add the D because you'll get that later.'

'The fat bird standing by the printers on the first floor. Don't want to shag, but could really do with a cuddle.'

7. Being told to 'get back in the kitchen' or 'make me a sandwich'

Recent years have seen a depressing return to retro sexism, particularly at schools and universities. As I've visited institutions up and down the country, countless students have reported coming up against 'old school' sexist comments like these, not just in social situations but also when trying to contribute in academic sessions or lectures. Rape jokes are also commonly reported.

8. Sexual assaults on nights out

A recent National Union of Students (NUS) study revealed that 37 per cent of female students had experienced 'inappropriate touching and groping' – acts defined as sexual assault under UK law. But so great is the social acceptability of these experiences that very few students would consider reporting them and many describe them as the norm.

9. Sexism in academia

It's not just club nights and initiations – female students come up against sexism in the classroom too. Two world-class debaters faced sexist abuse about their appearance and cries of 'Get that woman out of my chamber' while participating in a competition at Glasgow University union last year. And another recent NUS report found that female students were experiencing sexism across campus, including venues such as lecture halls and the gym.

10. 'Banter'

Perhaps worst of all, when female students try to challenge this litany of misogyny, they often come up against the defence that it's just 'banter', it's all just an 'ironic' joke. It's hilarious to rank women out of ten and laugh about raping them and post anonymous public judgements of their appearance online because nobody really means anything by it! The defence is an incredibly effective silencer, branding anybody who dares to complain as uptight or lacking a sense of humour. But the truth is, it shouldn't be possible to write a ten-point list of the abuse women have to brave in the process of learning. There's nothing funny about it at all.

Originally published 10 October 2014

SEXISM IS STILL SEXISM WHEN IT DOESN'T MAKE THE NEWS

A Texas advertising company, trying to show how realistic the stickers they make for the backs of trucks could be, decided that the best possible way to prove it was to create one that appeared to show a kidnapped woman tied up and lying in the back. Owner Brad Kolb told Texas news station KWTX that: 'It was more or less something we put out there to see who noticed it.' Because, really, what is violence against women if not a hilarious, attention-grabbing gimmick?

KWTX later reported that Kolb burned the sticker after an angry public response, which can only make one wonder at what point people are finally going to realize that this level of sexism is unacceptable before they go through with it, rather than after taking it round the block a few times and gauging the response. There shouldn't need to be a backlash every time an incident like this occurs for people to realize that violence against women isn't a suitable marketing tool.

Examples such as this show just how ingrained sexism is in our society. Over at the *Washington Post*, Richard Cohen produced a column whose title alone pretty much says it all: 'Miley Cyrus, Steubenville and Teen Culture Run Amok'. Yes, that's right folks, he did indeed conflate girls dancing and 'teen culture' with the brutal rape and subsequent online abuse of a teenage girl. He goes on to discuss the *New Yorker* account of the Steubenville rape, saying 'Cyrus should read it' and later adds, 'acts such as hers not only objectify women but debase them'. Reading the piece, you can see that Cohen actually means to criticize the misogyny of teen culture, and the inhumane treatment of the Steubenville victim. But by laying the blame for this at the door of Cyrus and, implicitly, other teenage girls who choose to be confident in and explore their sexuality, he himself does exactly what he accuses Cyrus of – he deals a serious blow to the women's movement or, indeed, any movement towards justice for victims of rape.

And these were just the more high-profile sexist moments of the past seven or so days. This is without even going into the online columns tearing down Kate Middleton because, the *Daily Mail* complains, 'Since giving birth, the Duchess's hair has looked rather worse for wear.' Without even mentioning the advert for HGV drivers that appeared on the massive online job website Reed, which not only precluded the possibility any woman might have the audacity to have the relevant licence and apply for the position, but was also entitled: 'NEED TO GET MORE TIME AWAY FROM HER INDOORS??' It's without even going into the fact that attendees at the TechCrunch conference in San Francisco had to sit through a presentation extolling the virtues of a new 'Titstare' app. (Does what it says on the tin.)

Yes, Reed removed the job advert after a barrage of complaints; yes, TechCrunch issued an apology, but once again the public acceptability of sexism meant these measures only came after the damage had already been done – when really these incidents shouldn't be happening in the first place.

Bear in mind that these are just the stories you hear – the ones that make the news – they don't even begin to scratch the surface of the individual, daily battles women and girls are facing against insidious, normalized sexism. The stories that are reported to the Everyday Sexism Project in their thousands every single week. Like the woman who was excused from jury duty on a rape trial this week, only to have the barrister ask her to stay behind because it's 'nice to have attractive ladies in court'. Or the girls who simply wanted to walk home from school in their uniform, the youngest aged just eleven, only to face beeps and catcalls and men shouting thoughtful advice such as 'get back to school, slag'. The woman who struggled to get on her plane at the airport because she had entered her title as 'Dr', and the booking system had automatically converted it to 'Mr'. The 16-year-old who was told 'girls can't do science' in her chemistry class, and the woman who wanted to apply for a PhD but was told to 'focus on getting your MRS degree first'. And, most ironic of all, the woman who attended an oil conference that had both a stand to attract more women into the industry and a bevy of 'bikini babes' wandering around aimlessly to attract male customers.

Originally published 13 September 2013

THIS IS RAPE CULTURE – AND LOOK AT THE DAMAGE IT DOES

What do we mean when we say 'rape culture'? You may have heard the term used recently. It describes a culture in which rape and sexual assault are common (in the UK over 85,000 women are raped and 400,000 sexually assaulted every single year). It describes a culture in which dominant social norms belittle, dismiss, joke about or even seem to condone rape and sexual assault. It describes a culture in which the normalization of rape and sexual assault are so great that often victims are blamed, either implicitly or explicitly, when these crimes are committed against them. A culture in which other factors such as media objectification make it easier to see women as dehumanized objects for male sexual purposes alone.

It's part of rape culture when 'I'm feeling rapey' T-shirts are put up for sale on eBay. It's part of rape culture when a child victim of sexual abuse is accused of being complicit and somehow 'egging' on her abuser in the court case against him. It's rape culture that makes it so hard for male victims to speak out, too, because hand in hand with the dismissal of rape as a hilarious joke goes the stigmatization of male rape victims as effeminate, impotent or non-existent.

Sometimes it's hard to recognize or understand rape culture without hearing real-life examples of how it impacts on everyday lives, starting from an incredibly young age:

@JillNicholls01: #followed home from primary school by gang of boys saying they'd rape me – didn't know what it meant but was scared – ran.

@TashaHugs: Overheard young boy on bus saying – 'I'll rape your mum so bad she can't walk'. Sickening!

@ShrutiSardesai: Can't go out for walks around my house bc routinely harassed, called names, and told that I need to be raped. Lovely stuff.

@Lethal_Brows: My co-worker was walking me to my car after my closing shift, I thanked him and he laughed & said he could rape me right now.

And the idea of rape becomes fair game for public jokes:

@AngelaBarnes: Genuine chat up scene unfolding on this train:

> Boy: do you have a rape alarm?
> Girl: yes
> Boy: shame

I despair for humanity.

Rape culture suggests that men have a 'right' to women's bodies, thus undermining the concept of consent:

> @TheUrbanDryad: Guy I used to go out with decides he wants to restart stuff between us. When I decline he threatens to rape me #ShoutingBack

This leads to common misconceptions about women 'asking for it' or 'wanting it', even if they explicitly say otherwise:

> @chazzyb31: At a party with bf, met his friend & pregnant gf. Friend follows me into toilets & says he's going to rape me bcs I want it.

> @Twinklecrepe: I was raped by a co-worker. I told my boss about it; she said it wasn't rape and implied I actually wanted it.

This leads to public speculation about whether victims' dress or behaviour could be to blame for their own assaults:

> @wyvanekk: two girls in my class were talking about how you'd only have yourself to blame for getting raped if you wore a short skirt.

> @Scathach_81: A former magistrate blames short skirts for rape on #bbctbq Welcome to 21st century Britain. #VictimBlaming

@Wolf_Mommy: When a man told me
breastfeeding my baby in public is going to
get me raped.

This shifts all the focus on to victims, while perpetrators are
not addressed at all:

@Sarah_Watsons: ever since I was little my mum
told me how to not get raped but I have never
heard her once tell my 2 brothers not to rape.

Rape culture can permeate every area of a woman's life, from
the pavement:

@grrumblecakes: And FURIOUS that there
are people alive who think threatening to
rape me on my way to work is a funny joke
#everydaysexism

To the workplace:

@adorrissey: upon hearing I was 19 and a
virgin, my co-worker suggested I 'needed to
get raped'.

From the classroom:

@EllenSteenkamp: At age 11 classmate on school
trip stated that 'no one would rape me anyway
cuz I'm too ugly'. Others only laughed at that.

To our own homes and families:

> @kyleisonline: bought an open back t shirt for
> a concert a month ago; my father told me the
> shirt screamed 'rape me'.

As the word starts to lose its meaning, it becomes harder and harder to object to rape culture:

> @charliecat82: #LadCulture being told by an ex-
> boyfriend that he'd like to rape me and then
> he didn't get why I was angry.

Worst of all, the widespread and normalized nature of rape culture makes it increasingly hard for victims to speak out, as they learn to believe they won't be taken seriously, or are dismissed when they do:

> @AmandaLouDT: On a nearly empty metro 4
> men shouted they wanted to rape me. Scary
> but we're not meant to make a fuss so didn't
> tell anyone

> @Frostbite___: I was 15 & my rape happened
> at a party. Never reported it because I knew
> I would get blamed & no would believe me.
> #RapeIsRape

@chitranagarajan: #ididnotreport because I
thought I was overreacting – when being
followed by groups of men and threatened
with rape.

@Vidyut: the usual. RT @THELOUDERMOUTH:
When I told friends I was raped, they
said I 'should have been more careful'.
#shoutingback

The cycle is perpetuated as victims are silenced and blamed, the crime normalized and perpetrators completely ignored.

This is rape culture.

Originally published 14 February 2014

WOMEN ARE BEING ASSAULTED, ABUSED AND MURDERED IN A SEA OF MISOGYNY

Leighann Duffy, twenty-six, has died in hospital after being stabbed in front of her 6-year-old daughter. A 64-year old woman has been stabbed multiple times at a support centre for care workers in south London. An 82-year-old woman has been beheaded in a north London garden. Pennie Davis, forty-seven, has been found stabbed to death in the New Forest. Suhail Azam has been jailed for stabbing his estranged wife, Kanwal Azam, to death. These reports are from the past couple of weeks alone. You probably haven't seen them all listed one after another like that. But when we start to connect different pieces of information, or even just consider them side by side, we begin to see patterns and links between them.

For example, the *Evening Standard* reports that domestic abuse is on the rise, with Metropolitan Police figures showing 28,000 recorded offences in the twelve months leading up to June 2014. Meanwhile, the charity Women's Aid has been forced to issue an emergency appeal as the number of specialist refuges has declined from 187 to 155 since 2010. Frontline women's services are at 'crisis point'. On one day alone in 2013, 155 women, with 103 children, were turned away from the first refuge they approached.

The news is peppered with reports of women being assaulted, abused and murdered. The campaigner Karen Ingala Smith reports that so far this year, the rate of women killed through suspected male violence has been one every 2.38 days. We know that on average two women a week are killed by a current or former partner – 51 per cent of all women murdered in 2011 and 2012, according to the Office of National Statistics. Yet we continue to report these crimes, if they are reported at all, as if they are isolated incidents. We don't look at the bigger picture.

The reason we don't consider the abuse and murder of women to be a newsworthy epidemic is because we are used to it. We don't connect it to the backdrop of sexism and gender inequality. We continue to think of it as something 'other' and unusual that happens to women somewhere else; women who are victims of strangers and monsters, not men like the ones you know. Even though women are most likely to be assaulted in their own homes or workplaces. Even though there's a 90 per cent chance a victim already knows her rapist. Even though, statistically, one in four of the women you know has been or will be a victim of domestic violence.

Joining the dots between these incidents matters because it is only when we see the problem as a whole that we can effectively work to tackle it. It also matters that we acknowledge a widespread and serious trend of women being killed by men, and that we set this trend within the wider context of normalized and ingrained sexism and misogyny.

When I started the Everyday Sexism Project, people asked why I included incidents of rape and violence alongside testimonies of street harassment or media sexism. The answer is simple. They demonstrate a spectrum. Women aren't killed in a bubble. They're killed in a world that disenfranchises them, positions them as other and disadvantages them. They're killed in a society that sends the message, clearly and repeatedly, that they are sexual objects for men's gratification and possession.

The cultural elements that help to create these messages aren't the cause of violence against women, but they are the context in which it happens. They help perpetrators to see women as objects. They frame violence against women as titillating, funny or excusable. They help us to blame victims when they come forward. They hamper justice.

While we fail to join the dots, women are dying. This sounds like an exaggeration, but isn't. These are not isolated incidents. You know that two women a week on average are killed by a current or former partner, but here's another statistic you might not have heard. Every day, according to the charity Refuge, almost thirty women attempt suicide as a direct result of experiencing domestic violence. Every week, three of them die.

Originally published 12 September 2014

Rape Is Not a Romp

In 1995 Private Cheryl James was found dead at Deepcut Barracks in Surrey with a gunshot wound to her head. She was just eighteen years old. A coroner later ruled that the wound was 'self-inflicted', and described the atmosphere at the barracks as 'sexualized'. Reporting on the inquest, *The Sun* published an article entitled '"Suicide" Army girl locked in for romp', in which it described how: 'Deepcut soldier Cheryl James was locked in a room and chased by a sergeant trying to "have his way" with her.' This headline is part of a much wider problem of *Carry On*-style, titillating depictions of sexual violence.

When a US teacher was in court accused of raping an underage student in 2017, US news outlets reported on the case with headlines like: 'Married middle school teacher, 27, arrested for sex romps with her underage boy student'. In another case, a newspaper covered a story about rape and human trafficking under a sensationalist headline about a 'sex slave', placing the story on pages 4 and 5 next to a picture of a topless woman on page 3. When singer Kesha made an accusation of sexual abuse against a producer, American talk-show host Wendy Williams discussed the case on her show, saying: 'If everybody complained because somebody allegedly sexually abused them ... then contracts would be broken all the time.'

After Hollywood producer Harvey Weinstein was accused of sexual harassment, assault and rape by dozens of women, *The Times* ran an article by Giles Coren that reduced the issue to PC gone mad, lamenting the fact that putting kisses at the end of emails could now 'end my glorious career'.

In December 2015, Daniel Holtzclaw was convicted of multiple counts of rape, sexual battery and other charges. A police officer, Holtzclaw had preyed on thirteen black, mostly low-income women, deliberately targeting those with criminal records or a history of drug use or sex work. But this didn't stop sports outlet SB Nation from publishing a 12,000-word apologia for Holtzclaw some two months after he had been found guilty. The article was titled 'Who is Daniel Holtzclaw?' The subheading answered not 'Rapist', but 'Linebacker'. The piece, peppered with self-aggrandizing quotes from Holtzclaw himself, painted him as a tragic figure who lost everything, describing him as 'quiet and reserved', a 'workhorse' with a 'keen sense of humour'. Despite Holtzclaw's conviction, the profile followed in a long tradition of similar media coverage, deliberately encouraging reader sympathy for the perpetrators of sexual violence and entirely glossing over the impact on victims. Part of the problem is the overwhelmingly white, male lens of front-page reporters – an internal report into the Holtzclaw debacle by SB Nation revealed its editorial staff to be 89 per cent male and 87 per cent white. Women write just over one-fifth of UK front-page newspaper articles and 84 per cent of those articles are about male subjects or experts. And when women do make the news, it is more likely to be because of their appearance or love lives than their achievements and opinions. So it is little surprise that our media continues to perpetuate sexist stereotypes, to belittle and blame victims of discrimination and to depict sexual violence irresponsibly.

When it comes to feminism, the media, which could play such a positive role in advancing gender equality, too often deliberately stands in its way. Women who try to create change are branded 'feminazis' in front-page headlines, feminist campaigners are mocked as humourless harpies and television 'debates' are set up to provide a national platform for known misogynists in the name of 'balance'.

Such treatment of misogyny risks sending the message that it is subjective and defensible, making the uphill battle for equality feel just a little bit steeper.

A CYCLE OF VIOLENCE: WHEN A WOMAN'S MURDER IS CALLED 'UNDERSTANDABLE'

I can think of many words to describe the murder of a woman by her own husband. 'Understandable' is not one of them. Yet this is the word that Dr Max Pemberton chose to use when he weighed in on Lance Hart's recent murder of his wife, Claire, and their 19-year-old daughter, Charlotte. Writing in the *Daily Mail*, and referencing the recent breakdown of the Harts' marriage, he said:

'Of course, such men are often motivated by anger and a desire to punish the spouse. But while killing their partner as an act of revenge may be understandable, for a man to kill his children (who are innocent bystanders in a marital break-down) is a very different matter. I believe it is often a twisted act of love, as the man crassly believes that the crisis in their lives is so great that the children would be better off dead.'

In this short extract, Pemberton describes the 'understand-able' murder by a man of his own wife as a 'very different matter' to his killing his child – an 'innocent bystander' – implying guilt on the part of the wife. He seems to suggest that, by ending their marriage, Claire had – at least in part – brought her death upon herself. Later referring to men who kill their own children, he goes on to use the phrase 'act of love', implying that perpetrators of such crimes are overtaken by passion – that such men should not necessarily be held fully responsible. Pemberton admits that 'there is often no evidence that men who kill their children have an identifiable mental illness', and yet later writes: 'And while it is, inevitably, hard to sympathize with such men, psychologists are divided as to whether they can be held truly culpable for their actions.'

Meanwhile, the *Telegraph* ran an article that opened: 'A father of three who gunned down his wife and 19-year-old daughter before killing himself had been upset following the breakdown of his marriage, it was claimed last night.' The article went on: 'Friends of the pair said they believed Lance had been struggling to move on with his life following the breakdown of the marriage, but they were still deeply shocked by the incident.' Those little words 'but' and 'still' suggest, powerfully, that the circumstances might somehow make Hart's actions more understandable, or even expected.

What's more, the piece went on to praise Hart, featuring vox pops from neighbours saying what a 'very, very nice guy' he was, describing him as 'full of the joys of spring' and giving irrelevant details about his DIY skills. The article contained no such quotes praising Hart's victims, Claire and Charlotte.

This is not just a matter of semantics. The way our media reports male violence against women can have a huge impact on societal perceptions of the problem. As Polly Neate, the chief executive of Women's Aid, says: 'The reporting of this case is deeply irresponsible because it minimises the culpability of Lance Hart, portraying him as an equal victim in a tragic case, rather than a man who chose to kill his wife and daughter. The phrase "twisted act of love" is particularly harmful, and shows why journalists need robust training on domestic abuse and homicide. Unless the lives of Claire and Charlotte are considered more important than some of the so-called "reasons" Lance killed them, we will never move to a culture that values women's lives enough to make them safer.'

Perhaps most worryingly of all, media responses such as those described above actively relieve perpetrators of responsibility and, by failing to set such incidents like this within a wider context of male violence, erase the societal problem they represent. In his *Daily Mail* article, Pemberton concludes: 'After any such incident, questions are inevitably asked about whether anything could have been done – if someone could have spotted the signs or intervened. Tragically, in most cases, experts agree that the answer is "no".'

Having completely divorced an incident from the systemic violence men inflict on women and girls, this is an unsurprising conclusion to reach. Which is why such narratives must be challenged, and why they are so dangerous. We must identify examples of male violence as just that: male violence against women. We must hold perpetrators fully accountable, and we must report responsibly on these cases. Only then will we as a society be able to recognize that, in fact, there is so much more that could be done.

Originally published 26 July 2016

RAPE IS NOT A PUNCHLINE – OR A
WAY TO SELL CHRISTMAS PRESENTS

Thirty-eight per cent of adults in the UK hear jokes about sexual assault or sex offenders regularly, according to a new survey by OnePoll. The nationally representative study of 1,000 British adults found that a quarter of men and 11 per cent of women said they had made this type of joke themselves.

The poll disproves the notion that these attitudes towards sexual violence are dying away. It found that 71 per cent of 18–24-year-olds have made a rape joke or flippantly used the word rape, and 88 per cent of respondents in this age group were familiar with the term 'frape', or Facebook rape, which is usually used to describe the act of logging into somebody else's Facebook account and posting using their profile. Thirty-six per cent of people aged 25–34 reported that they frequently hear the word rape used to mean 'beat in some form of competition'.

The results come amid a flurry of recent high-profile cases where companies have been forced to apologize after using rape, or appearing to allude to sexual assault, in festive advertising. A Singapore-based online retailer, SuperGurl, acknowledged it had 'made a mistake' after advertising its Black Friday sale with the slogan 'rape us now'. The department store chain Bloomingdale's apologized for its holiday advert, which featured a young man creepily eyeing a laughing young woman beside the slogan: 'Spike your best friend's eggnog when they're not looking'. This follows on from controversy last Christmas about a rape-themed Christmas T-shirt available for sale online, and a reference to chloroforming your partner in a 2012 Virgin Mobile US Christmas advert.

It isn't a coincidence that these cases seem to spike in the holiday season, when consumer culture reaches fever pitch. Such adverts, alongside the use of female bodies to sell unrelated products, promote the idea of women as consumable objects, there for the taking, with their own autonomy and choice conveniently left out of the picture. The fact that rape is seen as an acceptable topic to joke about, and use as a hook to sell products, reveals our social normalization of the concept – a phenomenon also described as 'rape culture'.

It is a difficult topic to discuss. Objections to rape jokes are frequently dismissed by those who argue that they represent a form of free speech, or those who point out that there is no evidence to prove a direct link between objectifying or sexually degrading images of women and sexual violence.

In fact, there is evidence of some links between the portrayal of women as sexual objects and attitudes that underpin violence against women and girls. The government-commissioned Sexualisation of Young People review found evidence to suggest a clear link between consumption of sexualized images, a tendency to view women as objects and the acceptance of aggressive attitudes and behaviours as the norm. And the 2010 report by the American Psychological Association Task Force on the Sexualization of Girls detailed links between sexually objectifying images of women and girls in mainstream media and significantly higher levels of acceptance of rape myths, victim-blaming, sexual harassment and interpersonal violence.

One particularly problematic aspect of the widespread and

flippant use of the word 'rape' is that it contributes to the idea that sexual violence is an acceptable topic about which to joke. Jokes in which rape victims are treated as a punchline are especially significant in a society in which only about 15 per cent of victims feel able to report serious sexual assault to the police. But while 87 per cent of those surveyed by OnePoll said they would never make a rape joke in front of somebody they knew to be a survivor of abuse, nearly a quarter of respondents said they felt it was acceptable to make these types of comments among friends. Yet when you tell a rape joke, statistically one in five women who hear you have experienced or will experience some form of sexual assault, whether you know it or not.

The idea that those who object to rape culture represent a threat to free speech is, ironically, a form of silencing in itself. There is a significant difference between expressing concern about rape jokes or images objectifying women and suggesting that all such content should be 'banned'. Indeed, it is unlikely that any kind of censorship would be particularly successful, as the problem lies as much with underlying attitudes as it does with the adverts or jokes themselves.

The feminist endgame is not to publicly punish everybody who makes a rape joke, or ban every advert that uses rape as a titillating way to sell products. It is to create a society in which it would never occur to anybody to do either in the first place.

Originally published 8 December 2015

WOLF-WHISTLING IS NOT THE STORY HERE – OUR REACTION TO SEXUAL HARASSMENT IS

A 23-year-old digital marketing co-ordinator has reported a group of builders to the police for sexual harassment. Every morning on her way to work, Poppy Smart faced gestures, disrespectful comments and wolf whistles – the builders would even come out of the site to whistle as she passed them and, on one occasion, one of the men deliberately blocked her path. Smart described the behaviour as 'incredibly intimidating' and said it had led her to consider changing her route to work. After a month, she reported the behaviour both to the firm who employed the men and to the police. The police investigated, but dropped the case when Smart was satisfied it had been handled internally.

This week, the case hit the headlines, sparking a wide range of responses. Though many later spoke out in support of Smart's decision, the initial response on social media seemed to be predominantly ridiculing or criticizing her. Elsewhere online, trolls made predictable contributions: 'What she needs is a bit of cock. That'll sort her out!' These responses have perhaps in part been elicited by the way in which the story has been covered. Although most articles made it clear that Smart involved the police only after experiencing a range of harassment every day for a month, the headlines pushed the wolf-whistling to the foreground.

BBC's *Newsbeat* reported the story under the headline: 'Woman goes to police over wolf whistles'. The *Metro* headline stated: 'Woman calls the police after being wolf-whistled at by builders'. The front page of the *Daily Mail* read: 'Girl calls in police after wolf whistles from builders'. One article even opened with the words: 'Police were called in to investigate a construction firm after a 23-year-old woman accused builders of sexual harassment – for WOLF-WHISTLING.' Several radio and television shows, including Channel 5's *The Wright Stuff* and ITV's *Loose Women* held debates on whether or not wolf-whistling should be made a crime.

Many of the discussions involved commentary on Smart's looks. One article highlighted the fact that she was childless and unmarried. Some news outlets used pictures that seemed to have been taken from Smart's social media accounts, showing her posing for selfies wearing a low-cut top – a decision it's difficult not to interpret as a snide suggestion that she might have somehow been 'asking for it'.

What all this seems to suggest is that, as a society, we are more concerned about, and outraged by, a young woman's audacity in standing up to sexual harassment than we are about the month-long, everyday campaign of verbal abuse she endured on her walk to work. The very fact that a story like this is set up as a juicy back-and-forth debate suggests that a woman's right to be treated as a human being is still being called into question. We have still not conclusively agreed that women have the right to walk the streets, wearing whatever they choose, without being shouted and whistled at.

Sarah Green, acting director of the End Violence Against Women Coalition, questions the media's 'cynical framing' of 'a story with lots of detail and angles'. 'Some of the newspapers have wilfully misrepresented what happened and created an impression of someone who responded disproportionately to something she should just ignore – that isn't what happened. She was left with few alternatives. [People] want to look at the victim's behaviour, not the abuse she endured,' Green continues. 'This denial goes with every form of violence against women, including domestic violence, rape and female genital mutilation. We have to ask: what does that mean? Because [the response] isn't comparable for other types of crime.'

A case in point: many commenters have focused on the fact that they felt Smart was wasting police time. Philip Davies, a Conservative MP currently seeking re-election in the West Yorkshire constituency of Shipley said: 'I would have thought the police have better things to do.' And on her BBC London radio show, Vanessa Feltz said: 'We take seriously people feeling harassed or threatened or intimidated – of course I do, I've got two daughters . . . but I just don't know how seriously this ought to be taken.' Feltz continued: 'Some people would say, if you don't like it, then cross the street or get a bit more robust . . . You don't think that your discomfort is worth using up valuable police time.'

In reality, though, we are hardly facing an epidemic of self-righteous women wasting police time with unimportant issues. In fact, the opposite is true. Many young women I have spoken to have endured groping and unwanted touching that falls squarely under the UK law on sexual assault, but would never dream of reporting it to the police because we live in a world in which it is considered a normal part of being a woman, or 'just a bit of banter'.

In fact, Smart was fully within her rights to involve the police. Assistant chief constable Garry Shewan is national police lead for stalking and harassment. He points to the contents of the Protection Against Harassment Act, as well as the Public Order Act, as evidence that 'It is not only unacceptable for someone to disparage, insult and offend someone in this way, but it can be against the law.' He continues: 'Just because some-one somewhere has a personal opinion that wolf-whistling and boorish behaviour is "fun" and not criminal does not make it right – try living with the day-to-day drip, drip feeling that someone is acting in a way that causes you fear and knowing that they just don't care about the impact on you.'

Clearly, there is a debate to be had about what constitutes behaviour likely to cause someone distress, but it strikes me that the most useful voices to listen to if we want to find out are those of the people experiencing harassment on a regular basis. From the response to Smart's brave stand, it seems even that simple step is a milestone we have yet to reach.

Originally published 29 April 2015

CALLING A WOMAN SEXY:
ACCEPTABLE OR NOT? HOW NOT
TO DISCUSS THE TRUMP TAPES

When is a news story just a news story? And when does it become a 'debate'? It's a difficult question to answer, particularly for harried researchers and editors on tight budgets, and tighter deadlines. But the answer matters, because it dictates how any given topic is framed for an audience and, consequently, the way in which the public engages with it.

When I first heard Donald Trump's taped comments that surfaced last week, I was most struck by the complacency with which he boasted about being able to commit sexual assault because of his status as a powerful, famous man. (Trump said: 'I don't even wait. And when you're a star, they let you do it; you can do anything . . . grab them by the pussy.') It was a hierarchy with which many women are familiar. So, too, are we horribly accustomed to the 'harmless talk' excuse he tried to use in the aftermath of the tapes' release. But, this time, the excuses didn't seem to be working. Even men famous for their own misogyny, men who had turned a blind eye while Trump made sexist, racist and Islamophobic comments in the past, seemed to have decided that his words were indefensible.

So it was something of a surprise to be asked to take part in a conversation on Radio 4's *Today* programme that ended up responding to the tapes by asking whether men need space to discuss women in sexual terms, and whether certain types of 'compliments' are acceptable. Those are valid questions in their own right. But to frame a discussion of Trump's remarks in those terms risks downplaying and mitigating the very serious nature of what he said, playing right into the hands of his own 'locker room' banter excuse. Indeed, it even required the presenter to ask at one point that we set aside the most serious element of Trump's words in order to focus on the rest: 'If you put that on one side though, the specific part of what he was taped saying that was obviously to you about assault, and you take the rest of it, is the rest of it acceptable?' I asked the presenter which bits he meant by 'the rest of it' – perhaps Trump's description of a woman as a bitch, or his graphic and misogynistic description of her breasts? He responded: 'So it's all the same, any description that objectifies a woman is an assault?'

Later he said: 'The serious issue ... is whether or not in 2016 it's acceptable for men together to talk about women in a sexual manner without feeling guilty about it.' It boiled down to the question: calling a woman sexy – acceptable or not? I would argue that perhaps that wasn't, in fact, the serious issue at hand.

Comments as shocking as Trump's require a less sympathetic media response, especially in light of the reality of sexual violence – 400,000 women are sexually assaulted in the UK annually, with one in five women experiencing some form of sexual offence in their lifetime. And, in a country where sexual violence is enormously under-reported and victim-blaming is rife, the framing of debates such as these not only sends a strong message to survivors about how their experiences are viewed, but also risks inadvertently validating those who hold views like Trump's. Broadcasters have a power over public opinion, and presenting something as 'up for debate' leads listeners to believe there are two equally valid sides to the story. Sometimes there aren't.

This is not to suggest that debate isn't healthy, or that difficult topics shouldn't be openly tackled. Of course they should. But this can be done in a way that doesn't imply equal validation of those inciting and opposing something like sexual assault. There are certain serious events and issues simply reported as news stories, or condemned in the media without the need for a 'devil's advocate' argument. The question is, who decides what is 'beyond debate'? It often feels as if issues around sexism and sexual violence are presented as even, two-sided questions even when what is discussed is extreme. And sometimes 'debate' is artificially manufactured for the sake of creating a more controversial news item.

Such misinformation is similarly perpetuated by news outlets that frame issues such as 'Is it OK to grab a woman on the street?' as questions, when the law already tells us the answer. This isn't a problem restricted to any one programme or media outlet – and it is complicated by the real need for balanced reporting. But there are many ways to achieve balance, such as debating the different ways to tackle a problem, which don't have to involve undermining the problem itself. And there are times when, at victims' expense, it feels as if 'balance' is a thinly veiled euphemism for controversy, clickbait or catfight.

Originally published 11 October 2016

NO, WIVES 'WITHHOLDING SEX' ARE NOT TO BLAME FOR MALE VIOLENCE

Wives who don't have enough sex with their husbands are partly to blame for men committing sexual assault, according to an article published by the *Daily Mail*. The writer, Dr Catherine Hakim, claims that 'decent' husbands whose wives 'starve' them of sex are driven to affairs and 'forced to seek relief elsewhere', resulting in 'a profoundly negative effect on our society – fracturing families and potentially leading to violence and crime'.

'Sexually starved men,' says Hakim, offering no evidence to back up this claim, 'are more likely to visit prostitutes, view pornography and, in the worst cases, even molest other women.' She later reiterates the supposed connection between sex-deprived husbands and sexual violence, writing: 'Men, as we know in our heart of hearts, will have affairs, or perhaps even worse, when faced with sexual starvation and the inevitable resentment that causes.'

Throughout the piece, the blame for men's behaviour is clearly and repeatedly placed with negligent wives, who are 'calling catastrophe into their lives' if they fail to have enough marital sex. But the author goes further, suggesting that such wives are also to blame for sexual violence befalling other women. She writes: 'More worryingly, there is little doubt, in my view, that sexual frustration can lead to assaults on women, though I am in no way excusing this behaviour.'

Yet excusing such behaviour is precisely the end result of a mainstream news website choosing to publish completely unsubstantiated claims repeatedly suggesting that men are pushed to commit sexual violence because their mean, frigid wives fail to sexually satisfy them. At no point is any comment made or judgement passed on the active choices of men who commit rape. The writer's stated credentials as a 'social scientist' and the use of unrelated statistics about sex in marriage create a deliberate veneer of scientific fact, though absolutely no proof is offered to substantiate the link between marital sex and male violence.

The conclusion readers are encouraged to draw is clear: poor, sex-obsessed men have no control over their own actions and no choice but to turn to affairs or sexual assault when marital sex is not available. No matter that such a ridiculous argument utterly relieves perpetrators of responsibility and is insulting to other men. Never mind that it ignores everything we know about rape, which is an act of power and control rather than sexual attraction. Or that it erases male victims and the existence of unmarried rapists. Or that it collapses in the face of the reality that 90 per cent of offenders are already known to their victims, suggesting that many women are still raped by their own husbands.

Indeed, the article also risks normalizing sexual pressure or even assault within relationships by reaffirming Victorian ideas about spousal responsibility for male sexual satisfaction. On the subject of affairs, Hakim says: 'What else are men who need sex regularly to do when married to an unsympathetic wife?' She appears to lament modern women's financial independence, writing wistfully: 'Though the days of women exchanging sex for financial security provided by their husbands are gone, we need to find new ways to trade our wants and needs for theirs . . . If he wants more sexual treats, tell him that the deal is you get more help with the washing up, a meal in a lovely restaurant or a new dress.' The notion that women might actually enjoy sex themselves, or even have the capacity to buy their own clothes and food, does not seem to occur to Hakim. And clearly it would be absurd to expect a husband to contribute to household chores without sexual bribery.

We live in a society where tens of thousands of women are raped annually and hundreds of thousands sexually assaulted, and where reporting rates remain dismally low – in part because of widespread victim-blaming and misconceptions about sexual violence. In that context, publishing such misogynistic, unsubstantiated nonsense to a wide audience could have a very real impact.

The people who read Hakim's article will include survivors of sexual violence and those who might come into contact with them, from friends and family to police officers and potential jurors. They will include women whose partners might be pressuring them into sex, or who might have experienced marital rape, or survivors who have been silenced and those who are weighing up whether or not to speak out.

But perhaps most worrying of all, the article will also be read by men, to whom it sends a clear message. You are not in control of your actions. You are not to blame. Your wife owes you sex, whether she feels like it or not, because you are a man and it is what you need and deserve. And if she doesn't oblige, it is reasonable or even inevitable for you to have an affair, or to sexually assault another woman (a natural progression). It's not your fault, she pushed you into it.

If anything risks having 'a profoundly negative effect on

our society ... potentially leading to violence and crime', it is not women who choose when they do and don't want to have sex. It is messages like these and the media outlets that choose to spread them.

Originally published 21 February 2017

HANDY GUIDES FOR
CONFUSED DUDES

For some men, who've lived their whole lives in a world that demands no inspection of their own privilege and who have little awareness of the harassment and discrimination experienced by women, all this is a lot to grasp. Many become very angry as a result, when equality measures are suggested. When I wrote an article for the *New York Times* about the potentially damaging impact of sex robots with a 'frigid' setting that would enable men to enact rape fantasies, one angry reader emailed me to protest. Surely I must concede, he railed, that it was better for him to 'force himself' on a robot than to rape his wife, who (I was shocked to hear) didn't often want to have sex with him. It struck me powerfully that he thought these were the only two options.

It's amazing how many men seem to confuse the idea of a woman's right to live an autonomous, harassment-free existence with a vicious attack on their own rights and freedoms. But those who claim that equality will somehow ruin their romantic advances must have a pretty strange idea of what flirting looks like.

In fact, men's misconceptions about feminism could fill an entire book on their own. On my way to a recent speech at a city firm, I accepted a seemingly kind stranger's offer to direct me. It turned out we were walking in the same direction, so he struck up a light, friendly conversation. When I explained that I was a guest speaker, he enquired as to the subject of my talk. When I replied 'equality and diversity', he was so horror-struck that he literally crossed the street to get away from me.

Perhaps unsurprisingly, this minority of men seems uniquely focused on their own personal interactions with women, whether in the workplace, online or in public. And their poor cries for help can be really quite pitiful: 'I'm a white man and I'm terrified I'm basically not allowed to say anything to a woman ever again,' bleated one poor soul on social media. Because this sounds like such a difficult plight (particularly in comparison with the sexual assault statistics he was commenting on), it seemed like some helpful how-to guides were called for.

EVERYDAY SEXISM: FIVE REASONS WHY MEN SHOULDN'T SHOUT AT WOMEN IN THE STREET

Over the past week, the Everyday Sexism Project has received an unprecedented number of stories from women experiencing harassment in the street. The 300 or so incidents this week are varied, and many go far beyond the common misconception of street harassment as just 'the odd catcall or wolf whistle here or there' ...

Here are just a few examples.

> @Izzy_Dickenson: Guy mutters 'slut' whilst passing me on stairs at Clapham Junction. I am quite blatantly dressed for a funeral.

> @richandgay: On the bus having things thrown and obscenities shouted at me by two young men asking for sexual favours. Delightful.

> @thejessicaraven: I'm so tired of people on the street calling me sexy. I'm six months pregnant, bro. You literally just need to leave me alone.

> @CathBailey: 200 f'ball fans outside pub in L'pool st chant 'get yer tits out 4 the lads' at 2 young women, then chase them. Police ignore.

@unicornhentai: Saw a drunk man catcall a
school girl and call her 'darling' while chasing
after her. It's unnerving.

@OtherPens: Crossing street in crowd, older
man grabs my hips in both hands while telling
me to walk faster. Shoves but doesn't let go.

@AndreaAuburn: just got followed home by two
neanderthals in a car shouting slut, slag, ugly
etc. etc. because I told them to leave me alone.

All this has prompted a burst of frustration over here at
Everyday Sexism HQ and since open letters seem to be all the
rage at the moment, we've penned one of our own . . .

Dear men who shout at women in the street,

Thanks for your latest. No, as it happens, I didn't have an
'ITCHY BEAVER!!!' but your acute observational skills are
bang on – I did let my hand brush momentarily across my
crotch as I went to get something out of my bag, so good
shout. The nice people who were in the florists next to my
house probably didn't need to hear it as you screamed out of
the window of your car though – I probably won't feel comfortable going in there for a while.

While we're corresponding, I thought I'd try to explain
why it's not okay to shout at women in the street, since our
repeated, clear assertion that we do not enjoy it and don't
consider it a compliment doesn't seem to have cleared things
up. Here are five simple reasons why.

1. It ruins nice things

Contrary to popular slander, we feminists aren't, in fact, saying that there's anything wrong with giving someone a polite compliment on the dress they're wearing, or nicely introducing yourself at a bar. We're asking you, please, to stop screaming about our tits at the top of your voices or declaring what you'd do to our vaginas when we've really given you no indication at all of our interest or availability. But, yes, the overwhelming volume of unsolicited attention that carries all the subtlety of an enquiry about the colour of our underwear is likely to make us more than a little wary of any advances. So, men who moan about feminists killing romance and forbidding flirtation, get angry at all the Neanderthal screamers out there instead – they're the ones really ruining it for the rest of you.

2. It won't work

Strange to have to spell this out, but the sheer volume of cases still occurring suggests that some catcallers still haven't grasped this simple pearl of wisdom. No woman, ever, has run sobbing after the car of the man who shouted about her fanny as he whizzed past, desperately begging him to take her to his lustful bed.

3. Your logic is flawed

You know when a woman declines or ignores your unsolic-ited, shouty advances, and you respond by screaming that she is a slut, a slag or a whore? In your outrage at the denial of your fundamental male right to harass, your logic has gone sadly askew. This doesn't add up. Think it through.

4. It's so passé

Shouting unsolicited sexual comments at passing women may once have been the route to prove your macho credentials to your peer group, but it's so 1990. The modern man has the right to be multifaceted, three dimensional and, would you believe it, even to respect women. Have a spark of imagination, won't you?

5. Karma

Beware the ultimate punishment for shouting at women in the street: karma. As these women's reports to @EverydaySexism show, it is less rare than you might think:

> @ragazza_inglese: Man just fell into a set of bins because he was too busy gawping at me to look where he was going. Karma #everydaysexism

> @FolieADarcy: Two guys whistling and honking at me from their car. Seconds later, they crashed it due to lack of concentration. #OwnFault

> @thejessicaraven: BAHA! Someone just shouted at me from a car and then crashed into a stop sign. #instantkarma

Originally published 10 October 2013

FLIRTATION OR SEXUAL HARASSMENT? HERE'S HOW TO TELL THE DIFFERENCE.

'Equality means never paying a woman a compliment' . . . said no feminist ever.

Amid the exciting recent surge of feminist activism and energy in the UK, a slight confusion seems to have crept in around the idea of battling sexual harassment. The general concern seems to be that by condemning sexual harassment and discriminatory behaviour, we will somehow accidentally sweep up well-meaning compliments and flirting in the melee and inadvertently do away with all sexual interaction.

Well, there's no need to panic! Feminism simply means wanting everybody to be treated equally, regardless of their sex. It's as simple as that. And no part of that definition maligns or 'bans' flirting, telling somebody they look nice or going at it like joyfully consenting rabbits in whatever style, location, position or combination of partners your heart desires.

What it does mean is that women shouldn't be scared to walk down the street; shouldn't be faced with intimidating and aggressive sexual shouts from cars and vans; shouldn't be treated as dehumanized sex objects; shouldn't be made to feel that men have an inherent entitlement to their bodies in public spaces.

Strange though it seems to have to keep reiterating it, the difference between sexual harassment and flirting is really fairly clear. It's actually quite insulting to the vast majority of men to suggest that they aren't perfectly capable of knowing the difference between complimenting someone, starting a flirty conversation and harassing them. The clue is in the name: harassment. And if you're hoping to end up in bed with someone, of whatever gender, it's really in your interests to steer clear of harassing them, as it's likely to be fairly unhelpful to proceedings.

I think very few men would be concerned, upon reading through the page after page of stories we have collected from women screamed at, pursued, groped, licked, touched, appraised, scared and frustrated by street harassers, that combating these things might somehow interfere with their personal pickup style.

But for those still in doubt, you could always run through this handy checklist of questions:

- Is the way in which I'm making this advance likely to scare or alarm the person?
- Has the person already made it clear to me that they are uninterested in my advances?
- Does the speed at which my vehicle is moving rule out any likelihood of a response to this advance?
- Is this 'advance' actually just a shouted and uninvited assessment on my part of this person's attractiveness/body/genitals?
- Does the context of this situation (a job interview, for example) make a direct sexual advance offensive or inappropriate?
- Am I actually, all things considered, just being a bit of a dick?

If the answer to any of the above is 'yes', then perhaps what's happened here is that you have accidentally confused sexual harassment with a respectful sexual advance. In this case, I refer you to the advice of a lady on Twitter, who rather eloquently summed things up:

> @almostalady: Frankly, if your 'liberated sexual advances' are cock-blocked by the @EverydaySexism project, you're probably doing them wrong.

More seriously, though, to make the wounded assertion that everybody, men and women, must retain their vital libertarian right to make direct propositions for sex is to display rather a major ignorance of the circumstances in which many women experience such propositions, on a near-daily basis. When you've had 'Get your tits out love' or 'All right darlin', fancy a shag?' shouted at you across a busy street; when you've been angrily pursued with shouts of 'slag . . . slut . . . whore' simply for politely declining such advances; when you've been lecherously harassed in the workplace, or confronted with somebody who simply won't take no for an answer until the alternative 'ownership' of a boyfriend finally convinces them – when you've experienced all this and more, it can have a bit of an impact on how you respond to unsolicited sexual advances.

Yes, sometimes just a tad of caution might creep in. Is it too much to ask that you respect that context? Is it really all just too wearisome to have to go that extra mile in your approach to reassure the person you're flirting with that you're not harassing them?

And if your answer is yes – if you are so frustrated by the atmosphere created by our gender imbalanced society in which such a large proportion of women experience harassment, and by the annoying caution that this engenders in some of your female flirting targets, guess what? The people you need to blame for that, the people you should be getting angry with, are the harassers. They are the ones ruining your fun and cramping your style – not feminist women and men who call out such behaviour when it happens.

Telling us that not all men are sexist or perpetrate harassment is preaching to the choir – the Everyday Sexism Project has received the most overwhelming support from men all over the world. We actually celebrate their awesomeness pretty regularly too.

But if you want to carry on making the point that many men are absolutely on the side of gender equality, you need to put your money where your mouth is. And in this case, that means stepping back, seeing the bigger picture and throwing your weight behind those battling sexual harassment, not moaning about the comparatively minuscule impact the widespread oppression of women might be having on your own personal sex life.

Originally published 10 April 2014

HERE'S HOW TO TALK TO WOMEN
WEARING HEADPHONES –
WITHOUT BEING AN IDIOT

Another week, another helpful, instructive article for the modern single man. This week: 'How to talk to a woman who is wearing headphones' – a topic only surpassed in its brilliance by other recent gems such as 'Seventeen killer mistakes a girl should never make on the first date' and 'Thirteen little things that can make a man fall hard for you'.

The internet abounds with such guides, most of which might more accurately be retitled 'How to be a complete jackass and ruin all chance you might ever have had of a relationship' or 'How to personify every outdated gender stereotype about relationship roles in ten easy steps'.

Glamour magazine's 'Thirteen little things' counselled women to answer the door naked, wait with a cold beer when a man steps out of the shower, sit quietly by his side while he watches his favourite TV show and (my personal favourite) let him 'solve your petty work problem'. Excellent advice for aspiring home-help robots or faithful canines; not so much for twenty-first-century women who don't despise themselves or want to burn everything.

Metro's 'Seventeen killer mistakes' list included helpful tips for how not to behave on a first date, such as 'There is such a thing as too much make-up', 'Don't mention your parents', 'Let's not have sex on the first date' and 'Don't think it's sexist that we offer to pay the bill'. Women were also advised not to 'tell us to order what we feel like, then get a salad from the starters after we've just asked for a rump steak', a variation on the infinite and contradictory rules out there about whether a woman can or can't eat salad on a date. Thanks, internet!

The latest offering – 'How to talk to a woman who is wearing headphones' – advised men to attract the attention of said women using much the same approach as an alien trying to blend in without arousing suspicion.

1. Stand in front of her (with 1 m to 1.5 m between you).
2. Have a relaxed, easy-going smile.
3. If she hasn't already looked up at you, simply get her attention with a wave of your hand.

Wave your hand in her direct line of vision so she can't ignore it.

Swoon. Excuse me while I go take a quick cold shower.

While there may be some women out there who would be delighted at this approach and immediately request marriage, the majority (judging from the response on Twitter) might find it annoying, scary, entitled or just downright rude. Given the amount of time women already spend fending off unwanted sexual advances, and the fact that many actively use headphones as a deliberate tactic to avoid them, an instructional piece encouraging men to invade our privacy is pretty much the last thing we need.

Yet, apparently, modern daters are in desperate need of guidance. So here's an alternative list of simple tips on how to talk to/date/generally interact with a woman without being a total idiot.

- Try to think about a woman as if she were a real-life human person. If you would find it weird to have someone wave their hand in front of your face with a fixed smile as you walk to work, the chances are she might, too.
- Don't do things to women that you would find annoying if done to you. This includes, but is not limited to, making unsolicited comments about body parts, musing aloud about fornicating with them or shouting out ratings out of ten.
- If paying the bill on a first date is the entire basis for your masculine sense of self, get help. Consider counselling, or have a nice long chat about self-worth with a friend or colleague.
- You can't judge a woman on her weight AND get angry if she orders a salad – that's just counter-intuitive. Try to work out in advance which sexist stereotype is most important to you, and stick with it.
- Remember that judging us on whether or not we want to have sex on a first date is the absolute, number one, most guaranteed way to turn us on. Women just love those sexist societal double standards. Lots of sex ahead for you.
- Acceptable reasons to approach a woman with headphones in: if she's about to step into a puddle, dog poo or the path of an oncoming car. If she is on fire and has not yet realized it.
- Unacceptable reasons to approach a woman with headphones on: anything else. Don't. Stop it.
- When you find a helpful article about how to approach

women wearing headphones, first check whether it is published on a website that says it can teach you 'What to say to turn a woman on and make her want to have sex with you ASAP', followed by 'This is very easy to do. You've got to try it!' Also check if said website sells a 10-hour-long video called 'Get your ex back: super system'. Do not take advice about women from this website.

Originally published 30 August 2016

FEMINISM DOESN'T MEAN A BATTLE OF THE SEXES, BUT A COMMON GOAL FOR ALL

Looking out over a sea of hands on a recent school visit, I felt a warm rush of elation at the sight of every single pupil raising their arm to affirm that they were a feminist.

Except that's not quite what happened.

In fact, when I asked everybody who was a feminist to put their hand up, the result was a paltry scattering or hands – 20 per cent of the assembly hall at best. So I asked the pupils to raise their hands if they thought everybody should be treated equally regardless of their sexuality, and every hand in the room went up. I asked them if everybody should be treated equally regardless of skin colour and, again, the response rate was 100 per cent. Finally, I asked them to put their hand up if they thought everybody should be treated equally regardless of their sex. Everybody in the room raised an arm.

'If you have your hand up now,' I explained, 'then you're a feminist. That's what feminism means.'

Apart from a few horrified boys who snatched their hands down in dismay, the general reaction was one of bemusement. Several kids asked if boys were allowed to be feminists, and others protested that they couldn't possibly be, since feminism meant wanting women to defeat, overtake or generally beat men into submission.

It's not surprising that these outdated and false stereotypes persist, given their stubborn repetition in the media and across the internet. In fact, there seems to be a huge amount of anxiety about the current resurgence of feminism and what it might mean for men. In the past week alone we have seen wails that the sacking of Jeremy Clarkson points to an 'emasculated' BBC, articles proclaiming that UN statistics on sexual violence unfairly malign men, comment pieces that declare the 'real' everyday sexism in the UK to be against men; even Russell Crowe mourning 'the loss of traditional masculinity'.

What's strange is that often at the heart of this panic is an entirely false dichotomy. Such arguments suggest that tackling issues such as sexism, street harassment or domestic violence somehow precludes action on problems that disproportionately affect men.

The idea that the fight for gender equality somehow erases masculinity or disempowers men seems to be strangely insulting to any man whose sense of identity doesn't come from being offensive to women. Feminism doesn't mean doors can't be held open any more, or the end of flirting, or that men should never again pay a woman a compliment. That's simple human kindness we should all show one another, regardless of gender.

The idea that feminism must somehow result in either deliberate or collateral damage to men is simply not true. Almost every issue that feminists campaign about would have a positive knock-on effect for men. The entries to the Everyday Sexism Project reveal this with brilliant clarity – in the same week, we'll receive one entry from a man refused parental leave and ridiculed in the office for asking for it, and one from a woman who has been refused a promotion because she is considered a 'maternity risk'. We hear from girls who aren't allowed to join in football games and boys who are bullied for wanting to take 'girly' subjects such as art or drama. We learn of fathers congratulated for 'babysitting' their own children and mothers criticized for 'taking a night off'. Many of these problems are so obviously two sides of the same coin.

The same is true for many of the issues that men's rights activists raise as exclusively 'male' concerns, with the suggestion that feminism ignores these problems. Invariably, these include accusations of gender imbalance in the allocation of custody, or the fact that the male suicide rate is several times higher than it is for women. What they don't seem to realize is that these, too, are closely linked to the inequality that feminism seeks to address. If there is an unfair bias towards female carers, it likely stems from stereotypes about women being family-oriented and men being career-focused. It seems sensible to assume that at least some part of the gender disparity in suicide rates may be connected to the pervasive idea that men must be tough and strong, that boys don't cry and it's shameful for men to talk about their feelings or reach out for help. The flip side of this is the notion that women are overemotional, hormonal or hysterical. Tackling these stereotypes would be good for everybody.

It will slow us all down if people persist in peddling this outdated dogma that sets men and women up against each other. Of course, not all men are sexist, and not every woman will necessarily face sexism. Gender inequality has a negative impact on men as well as women, though its structural and ingrained nature (politically, economically, socially and culturally) does mean that women tend to experience its effects more frequently and more severely. There is a vital role for men to play in this battle, and it isn't as detractors or naysayers, but as allies, agents of change and beneficiaries. This isn't about men against women, it's about people against prejudice, and everybody needs to get on board.

Originally published 27 March 2015

SEVEN QUESTIONS TO ASK YOURSELF BEFORE JUDGING A PREGNANT COLLEAGUE

Rachel Reeves MP, shadow secretary of state for work and pensions, has said that she plans to continue her political career if her party comes to power while she is – gasp – pregnant. To read some of the comments and think pieces about this revelation, you might be forgiven for thinking that she had admitted an ambition to make bonfires of taxpayers' money.

The 'stupid woman' is 'setting the case for working women back by about fifty years' according to one column. Another spits that she is 'treating motherhood as a part-time obligation, almost a hobby', is not 'fit to represent women' and should be disqualified forthwith from 'ever making important policy decisions affecting women'. Fellow MP Andrew Rosindell fretted that she might not be able to give the job her 'full attention', arguing that 'people need to be put in the positions they can handle'.

Since when has being pregnant become a shocking and shameful act? For those who might still find the very common act of reproduction a bewildering minefield, here are seven handy questions to ask yourself before making judgements about somebody else's pregnancy . . .

1. Am I being patronizing to the pregnant woman?

'Have you thought this one through?' is one example of what not to say. Don't worry – the person intending to push a human being out of a very small hole and subsequently house and care for that small human for the foreseeable future has, in all likelihood, given it a bit of thought.

Worried about how they'll juggle childcare with their job? The chances are they are, too, but they've probably got a plan to make it work. Concerned they're not taking their job seriously enough? Relax – considering they're the one that's been doing the job up until now and are intimately acquainted with its challenges and demands, they've probably got it covered.

2. Am I treating it as an anomaly rather than a normal part of life?

Much of the criticism seems to stem from the idea that pregnant women are selfishly swanning off to satisfy their desire to 'have it all', to the detriment of taxpayers/business owners/neglected children (delete as appropriate). Let's stop and realize how ridiculous an idea that is. A child is not a luxury accessory, but a normal – though not, of course, essential – product of a human life.

Collectively dealing with the needs of pregnancy and parenthood should be built into the very fabric of our workplaces, businesses and societal ideas about careers, not bolted on as an afterthought. The experience of pregnancy and new parenthood shouldn't be treated as something shameful that women feel they have to hide in order to be seen as competent. For those who choose to stay in work it should simply be assumed that necessary support during and after pregnancy – such as flexible working hours, shared parental leave and on-site crèches – will be provided. It should be a national scandal that over 50,000 women a year lose their jobs as a result of maternity discrimination.

3. Am I making assumptions about the reasons for a woman's choices?

Is a mother who returns to work quickly really a selfish career-obsessive? In fact, she might just be passionate about her job, have a partner more readily able to take on childcare or not be able to afford more time off.

Is the woman who chooses to stay at home really a feminist failure, yummy mummy or dropout? Or might she have made a careful decision about what's right for her and her family? Might she have exercised precisely the kind of choice that feminists want women to have? Might prohibitive childcare costs have made the decision for her?

4. Would I say this to the father?

Worried that sleepless nights, nappy changes and general emotional exhaustion will take their toll on a new mum? They might, to an extent. In much the same way that illness, bad break-ups and family bereavements sometimes take a toll on all of us. But we don't suggest that people dealing with these problems should be sacked, do we? Sleepless nights are a natural part of life as a new parent. But fathers aren't deaf to babies' night-time screams.

They, too, are experiencing major life upheaval and the emotional roller coaster of early parenthood. Why is it that we don't discuss the impact a new baby will have on a man's work life?

5. Have I considered the impact that publicly debating this woman's fitness to work might have on her?

We should be so far beyond the indecency of creating a public 'debate' about someone's career competency on the basis of procreation. What kind of impact might it have on a person to see their work called into question by the comment police when they're continuing to kick ass in the workplace, even while lugging around the weight of a sack of potatoes, creating a new life and constantly battling the urge to pee?

In Reeves's case, as for other high-profile figures, the point is particularly pertinent, given the impact such chatter could have on voters' impressions of her performance.

6. Have I considered the fact that women may experience pregnancy differently?

#NotAllPregnancies wants to prevent women from being able to continue working. If you think pregnancy is by default a completely debilitating condition, check out Olympic athlete Alysia Montaño, who competed in the 800 m while in her third trimester; Amy Poehler, who brought the house down with a rap about Sarah Palin on *Saturday Night Live* while nine months pregnant; and Marissa Mayer, who took over Yahoo while twenty-eight weeks pregnant.

What's important is that we offer whatever help and support a woman needs, instead of making our own assumptions about what she will or won't be able to handle.

7. Am I expecting this woman to represent all women?

It is neither Rachel Reeves's nor any other woman's responsibility to represent all women in her life choices. We all have different needs and priorities – including single parents, same sex couples and adoptive parents – and different situations.

Choosing to continue working doesn't 'denigrate' or cheapen motherhood. Choosing to leave work to raise children doesn't fly in the face of feminism or let down other women. Continuing to hold a high-profile political position while pregnant doesn't fail the country. What does hold women back is acting as if we are a homogenous group, ignoring our right to make our own individual choices and asking stupid questions when we do.

Originally published 13 March 2015

HOW NOT TO TALK TO FEMALE NASA ASTRONAUTS

When Nasa astronaut and comparative physiologist Jessica Meir tweeted about entering the 'space equivalent zone, where water spontaneously boils' last week, one man, whose Twitter bio said he had once been to space camp, responded as follows: 'Wouldn't say it's spontaneous. The pressure in the room got below the vapor pressure of the water at room temp. Simple thermo.'

Naturally, Twitter responded magnificently, with other users queuing up to congratulate him on his expertise and asking him to 'please explain science in more detail to the tweeting astronaut'.

He wasn't alone. In recent months, there has been a spate of men stepping up to foist their own, less informed perspectives on far more qualified women. At a rally last week, Donald Trump got in on the act. When former aviation operations specialist and US Marine Corps veteran Rachel Fredericks, who suffers from PTSD, asked Trump what action he would take to 'stop twenty veterans a day from killing themselves', Trump's immediate response was: 'Actually, it's twenty-two.' Fredericks was left shaking her head as Trump cited statistics less up-to-date than her own.

This came only a month after astrophysicist Katherine J. Mack tweeted her distress about the damage being caused by climate change, only for a male blogger to suggest: 'Maybe you should learn some actual SCIENCE then.' Luckily, Mack had the perfect response: 'I dunno, man, I already went and got a PhD in astrophysics. Seems like more than that would be overkill at this point.'

But even her excellent retort wasn't allowed to go unchallenged. The man, not knowing when to quit, delete his Twitter account and reconsider his life choices, replied: 'Then you should ask for a refund because they failed to teach you the most basics of science.' When Mack fired back with further proof of her credentials, another male tweeter stepped in to instruct her: 'Katie, as much as its hilarious, let's not entertain the trolls.' Because it would have been too much to let the incredibly intelligent and qualified astrophysicist choose her own method of dealing with the problem.

Women in a wide variety of fields can encounter this problem, as Olympic cyclist Annemiek van Vleuten discovered when she had a serious crash during the women's road race in Rio. Tweeter Martin Betancourt offered her this generous advice: 'First lesson in bicycling, keep your bike steady ... whether fast or slow.'

Being corrected by less qualified men is a phenomenon reported by many women, particularly those with expertise in a male-dominated area. At the Everyday Sexism Project, we've heard from an IT worker whose less experienced male colleagues outlined basic computer functions to her in meetings, an engineer who had a man try to explain solar panels to her and a woman who dealt with a customer slowly spelling out her own company policies to her while calling her 'honey'.

There is a serious underlying issue here. These interactions are the visible manifestation of societal assumptions about women's inferiority in intellectual and professional situations. They represent the same ingrained stereotypes that lead to women being less frequently promoted or hired for certain jobs. The same issues are at play when women find themselves being spoken over in the workplace, when a client directs every question to a junior male colleague or when a woman makes a suggestion in a meeting and is ignored, only for the same idea to be voiced by a male colleague to loud agreement moments later. It is what writer Soraya Chemaly has described as 'good old-fashioned sexism expressed in gendered socialization and a default cultural preference for institutionalized male domination of public life'.

However, as Chemaly points out, the way to fix it isn't simply to suggest that women need to be more assertive, as we are often told. The problem doesn't spring from hesitant women wringing their hands and dithering until a heroic man rides in and provides an explanation. The aforementioned astronaut, astrophysicist, Marine Corp veteran and Olympic cyclist hardly fit that description.

No, it arises when men are brought up in a world that teaches them that their knowledge and opinions are worth more than those of a far more qualified woman. It happens when some men act on these ingrained assumptions. And its impact, particularly in the workplace, can go far beyond the initial annoyance. The only way to stop it is to change the narrative that sets up male contributions as superior in the first place, not to 'train' women to deal with it later on.

In the meantime, here is a good rule of thumb for over-enthusiastic men on Twitter to follow: if she's wearing a Nasa spacesuit, take a minute to consider whether you really want to tell her how to do her job. Or, as one tweeter put it, 'This lesson went well, I think. But you should have told her to smile more. Women love that.'

Originally published 13 September 2016

Harassment vs Free Speech vs Banter

'Freedom of speech' is one of the most misused terms in modern discourse, wrongly used to excuse, cover up or defend abuse. Bandied about like a kind of magical shield that defends the user against criticism, argument or reasoned debate, the term is often used inaccurately.

Free speech is not limitless. It doesn't enshrine anybody's right to abuse, to incite hatred or to threaten and terrify others. The right to speech is not the same as the right to be heard, to be given a platform or an audience. It isn't the right to force a woman to listen to and tacitly accept your misogynistic, bigoted slurs or your fantasies about raping or killing her.

Too often, the excuse is used as a carte blanche for social media platforms to shrug their shoulders and pretend their hands are tied. In reality, laws about freedom of speech don't apply on a private platform like Twitter or Facebook. Such companies can and do decide which content to allow and disallow, and seem to have little difficulty policing posts about breastfeeding, mastectomies and menstruation. So there should be similar action taken against the small number of people who use these platforms to terrorize and abuse others or, as charities such as Women's Aid have warned, in a worryingly increasing number of cases, to extend behaviours such as stalking and domestic violence.

Sadly, social media platforms' policies seem to be fluid and evasive, with many moderation decisions suddenly reversed after a particular story hits the headlines or causes a public outcry. Strange, considering how often it is implied these decisions have been made for grand ethical reasons like 'freedom of speech', that they can be so quickly changed when the risk of reputational damage arises. This is particularly problematic because the nature and demographics of mainstream media outlets mean that the stories picked up and thrust into the limelight most frequently feature attractive, white, privileged women. So women of colour and LGBTQIA social media users, already likely to receive worse abuse and be bombarded with multiple forms of online prejudice, find themselves less likely to see their cases elevated to public attention and therefore speedily or satisfactorily resolved.

Nor should 'freedom of speech' only apply to those whose speech we actually hear. We ought to consider, too, the lost sound of those who don't speak at all, because their voices are drowned out by the angry shouting of those demanding their own right to be heard. The teenage girls who disappear from social networks because it's not worth the abuse. The activists who become too tired of putting their head above the parapet. The non-binary folk and people of colour for whom certain kinds of speech, especially online, might result in physical danger too great to risk. Next time you hear someone bellowing about 'free speech', ask whose speech we actually get to hear and why.

ONLINE ABUSE AGAINST WOMEN: 'FREE SPEECH' IS NO JUSTIFICATION

Just over a month ago, while doing research for a book about sexism, I opened an internet browser, typed 'chat rooms for kids' into Google and clicked on one of the first links that appeared. There was no registration process, no age check – I just typed in a made-up username, and immediately chat windows started appearing on my screen. Within seconds I had over ten messages, almost every one of them reading: 'ASL?' I wrote back: 'What is ASL?' The answer came quickly: 'Age. Sex. Location.' I replied, claiming to be a 12-year-old girl from the US. The responses were immediate:

'Do you like sex?'

'Can I teach you?'

'Bra size?'

'Do you want to earn some extra pocket money?'

'Can I cu?'

While I hesitated, the messages quickly intensified: 'My dick is long and hard' . . . 'I am so horny' . . . 'My wet dripping dick'. I closed the windows. The whole thing took less than three minutes.

In the course of my work around violence against women and the forms it takes online, I've learned that it can get far more complicated – one expert recently told me about scenarios where men have sent messages to girls in chat rooms claiming to have uploaded a virus on to their computer . . . but they'll delete it on the condition of a video chat . . . if the girl does what she's told.

This week a Dutch children's charity carried out a very similar experiment on a much larger scale, using a computer-generated 10-year-old girl they named Sweetie. The results were chillingly similar, with 20,000 men contacting Sweetie over two months and 1,000 offering to pay her to carry out sex acts on a webcam. But the reaction of law enforcement agencies to the revelations has been notably muted – though the UK's National Crime Agency has agreed to look at the information passed on by the charity, a spokesperson for European policing agency Europol told Reuters: 'We believe that criminal investigations using intrusive surveillance measures should be the exclusive responsibility of law enforcement agencies.' No promise of more concrete action has yet been forthcoming. This has only confirmed what we already knew – when it comes to online abuse, women and girls are on their own.

The internet is a fertile breeding ground for misogyny – you only have to look at the murky bottom waters of Reddit and 4Chan to see the true extent to which it allows violent attitudes towards women to proliferate. But, crucially, it also provides a conduit that enables many who hold those views to attack and abuse women and girls from what they rightly perceive to be an incredibly secure position. Meanwhile, the police seem near-powerless to take action, social media sites shrug their shoulders and women are left between a rock and a hard place – simply put up with the abuse as a part of online life, or get off the internet altogether.

These are not just nasty comments or harsh criticisms – they are extreme, detailed and vitriolic threats of rape, torture and death. I have received messages detailing exactly how I should be disembowelled, which weapons could be used to kill me and which parts of my body should be raped. When I ignored the threats, they intensified and proliferated, finding out information about my family members and threatening to rape them instead. They are the kind of messages that race around your head at night when you try to sleep, no matter how much you wrote them off as empty scare-mongering during the day. They make you hesitate to post online and change the way you use social media. And nobody seems to be able to do anything about it. Of the three rape threats I reported to police in recent months, two cases have already been dropped because the police are unable to trace the perpetrators. When I went to the police last year with a pile of abusive messages, including rape and death threats, they said they were unable to trace the perpetrators, even though I was able to provide IP addresses. When I showed them a specific website where users were being encouraged to send me abuse and threats, the police said it was US-registered and therefore outside their jurisdiction.

Just like Sweetie and any other young girls her age venturing into shared online spaces, the answer seems to be an ambivalent shrug – this is just what happens to women online so you might as well get used to it. And woe betide you if you try to protest the apparent unfairness of that, because didn't you know that you are threatening free speech? Except that it's not a threat to free speech to suggest that once people have actually committed a crime (like threatening to rape or murder somebody, or trying to coerce a little girl into carrying out sex acts), they should be brought to justice for it. Threatening to rape somebody online is just as illegal as it is in a letter, or in person. Nobody is suggesting that the entirety of

Reddit or 4Chan should be shut down, objectionable as some parts of them are.

But it's also telling that in all this hand-wringing over free speech, nobody is talking about the free speech of the women and girls who, as long as this continues to go unacknowledged and unresolved, are effectively being driven out of online spaces altogether.

Originally published 8 November 2013

EIGHT THINGS NOT TO SAY TO SOMEONE FACING ONLINE ABUSE

The only thing nearly as demoralizing and frustrating as being bombarded with online abuse is listening to the things people repeatedly tell you when they find out you're experiencing online abuse. It's the reason that when *The Guardian* recently published its research into the tone and content of 70 million comments on its articles – and the methodology used – I couldn't bring myself to read the responses 'below the line'.

Sometimes, it's well-meaning – when people reassure you that there's no real risk, for example, they're trying to make you feel more secure. But at its worst, the way in which we respond to those experiencing online harassment risks normalizing it, isolating them further or implicitly blaming them for the abuse. Here are some of the most common responses I've heard:

1. I hate it when people disagree with me, too

Online abuse is not an intellectual squabble. In fact, it's marked by a total failure to engage with your argument. It's often characterized by personal attacks, sexual comments, racism, homophobia or transphobia and threats of physical violence or rape – none of which have anything to do with disagreement.

2. You know they're only trying to scare you, right?

Probably the most common reaction, but one that completely underestimates the psychological toll of trawling through strangers' fantasies about what weapons they would use to gut you, and in what order.

Online abuse can have a major psychological impact, whether or not you fear for your immediate physical safety. For many victims, online abuse does indeed spill offline, with their addresses or those of their family members shared widely (a practice known as 'doxxing').

If you're on the receiving end of hundreds of long, detailed, graphic threats, you can't help wondering whether just one person might follow through. And when you've received a detailed rape threat with an exact time and date in it, it's very hard not to start looking at your watch as the hour draws near, no matter how rational you are.

3. What did you say to annoy them?

People who respond like this imply that online abuse is at least partly the fault of the victim. They assume that it wouldn't have happened if you hadn't said something inflammatory or provocative. But this plays right into the prejudices of abusers, by casting feminist or anti-racist opinions, for example, as something extreme and challenging. Furthermore, we know that very similar posts made by accounts presenting as male or female get a very different reaction, so it isn't about what you say, it's about the prejudices of those responding.

4. Have you thought about shutting down your Twitter account?

Oh, gosh, no, that hadn't occurred to me, thank you! Silencing is the end goal of the majority of abuse. If you suggest that someone who is experiencing it shuts down their social media accounts or stops speaking out, you're suggesting their freedom should be curtailed because of someone else's abusive behaviour. In fact, you are unintentionally helping the abuser.

5. Have you reported it to the police?

The answer is yes, over and over again. In my experience, they are generally kind, supportive and take it seriously – although clearly this is not the case for everyone, as detailed in Lily Allen's account of harassment, which started on social media. But it takes a long time and a lot of mental energy to go through the process of reporting a crime like this and unfortunately ...

6. 'What's a Twitter handle?'

... was one of the first questions a police officer asked me when I was describing a recent spate of abuse and rape threats. Law enforcement has yet to catch up to the Wild West of the internet and we need to see both police and social platforms doing more to protect users.

7. It's just a sad middle-aged single man/a spotty teenage boy alone in his mum's basement

First off, this seems fairly offensive to the vast majority of teenage boys/single middle-aged men. Assigning any particular demographic to online abusers risks letting them off the hook, with implied societal reasons (and excuses) for their behaviour. What's harder, but necessary, to confront is that many of those who abuse online are people within our communities, families and friendship groups, not just 'weirdos' or outcasts.

8. Don't feed the trolls

Notice how many of these responses focus on policing victims' behaviour? No matter how well-meaning it might be, telling someone how they should respond plays into the idea that they are somehow responsible for provoking, or capable of preventing, the abuse. If you want to engage with so-called Twitter trolls, go for it. As Mary Beard has proved, in some cases, it works very effectively. If you want to switch off, that's okay, too.

It is tempting to try to respond to online abuse by telling the victim not to worry, or explaining how you think they could solve it. But this can often inadvertently reinforce the very narrative that trolls seek to create. It's better to respond with support, or to challenge the online harassment. Above all, we should focus on stopping online abuse from happening in the first place.

Originally published 19 April 2016

HOW VIDEO 'PRANKSTERS' ARE CASHING IN ON THE ABUSE AND HARASSMENT OF WOMEN

When 22-year-old student and writer Paulina Drėgvaitė headed to Trafalgar Square last week, she was simply planning to meet a friend in central London and enjoy the good weather. As she sat on the steps of St Martin-in-the-Fields, a young man approached her, told her it was 'national kiss day' and asked her to kiss him. She smiled and said, 'No, sorry, no.' Instead of accepting her answer, he demanded to know why. She answered: 'Because I have no desire to kiss you.' Again, he persisted, asking: 'What if I show you my nipple?' At this point, she told him to 'fuck off', and asked him what right he thought he had to speak to her in that way. Laughing it off with a sarcastic comment, he walked away.

It wasn't until the following day when a friend sent her a link to a Facebook video that she realized the man who had approached her was Jack Jones, a self-styled online 'prankster' with a Facebook following of almost 3.5 million people. Without her knowledge or consent, he had filmed his interaction with Paulina and used her as the punchline on a video titled 'National kiss day'.

The video, which ends with Drėgvaitė saying 'Fuck off', has since been viewed over 700,000 times and has 12,000 likes, 850 shares and more than 600 comments. To her horror, Drėgvaitė realized that hundreds of the comments focused on her, describing her as ugly, stuffy, stuck up, arrogant and dumb, calling her a snotty cow and a feminazi, and speculating about whether she was on her period.

'I was physically shaking,' says Drėgvaitė. 'I feel sick and violated. The video was put up without my consent and now thousands of people are calling me a fat cow because I refused to kiss a man I had no desire to kiss. Some people have advised me just to let it go, but I feel like this event is so symptomatic of the everyday sexism that women face: getting harassed in a public space and then being bullied because of it.'

Jones is just one of a host of online 'pranksters', mostly young men, whose videos often show them approaching, scaring or harassing unsuspecting women in public spaces under the guise of 'banter'. Often euphemistically described as 'social experiments', recent examples to hit the headlines have included YouTuber Sam Pepper's compilation of grabbing women's bottoms in the street and Brad Holmes's video showing his partner Jenny Davies in pain after using a tampon he had rubbed chilli on as a 'prank'. Though several sites removed the chilli video after campaigners pointed out it normalized relationship abuse, many mainstream media outlets continue to host it.

More and more vloggers are making money and enjoying notoriety built on the harassment or abuse of women. Regardless of whether or not some of the 'pranks' are staged, you only have to look at the thousands of comments on the videos to see that they are playing a part in perpetuating misogynistic and abusive attitudes towards women and normalizing harassment. With titles such as 'How to pick up girls' and 'How to get any girl's number', the videos often encourage viewers, implicitly or explicitly, to replicate the same tactics themselves. It is not uncommon for sexism and racism to intermingle in the harassment depicted.

Where the videos centre on a female partner, they veer uncomfortably close to the controlling and coercive norms that often mark an abusive relationship. One Brad Holmes video, for example, shows him slashing a piece of clothing he had bought for his partner with a knife in front of her and stamping on a brand-new set of hair straighteners while she begs him not to, because she fails to answer questions about history and football correctly. In another, with 10 million views, he cuts her hair without consent while she sleeps.

Soraya Chemaly, director of the Women's Media Center Speech Project, says: 'Pranks and jokes say a lot about what society thinks is acceptable and, unfortunately for girls and women, what's acceptable is high levels of physical aggression, denigrating humour and non-consent. You see that trifecta not only in the actions of harassers, who are socially supported, for example, by views and likes, but in the institutionalized policies of social media companies, whose policies tend to reflect mainstream norms.'

In many cases the women involved can be left, like Paulina Drėgvaitė, feeling frustrated and helpless. She reported the video to Facebook and asked for it to be taken down, but received a message in response saying that it did not contravene community guidelines. A spokesperson for Facebook has since said they were investigating both the 'National kiss day' and the chilli tampon videos.

While each of these videos is subtly different, as a whole there is something very troubling about the triumphant rise of internet stars who are dealing in the currency of female harassment and humiliation, with sexual success positioned as the ultimate goal. To legions of online fans, the message is clear: any woman is fair game; their presence in public space is an invitation for harassment and you don't need to take no for an answer.

Originally published 2 June 2016

CELEBRITY CONSENT: STOP BRANDING ATTACKS ON WOMEN AS 'PRANKS'

Picture the scene: a male celebrity is exiting an event when suddenly someone runs up to him, dodging his security team, and attempts to grab his wallet from his pocket. Reacting instinctively, the celebrity puts up a hand to stop the attacker, perhaps pushing them away or to the ground. Headlines relay the shocking event, many praising the 'action hero' for his real-life reflexes.

Yet while our sympathies would likely be firmly aligned with a famous man facing an attempted robbery, the reaction seems to be very different when female celebrities experience what amounts to attempted assault. While exiting a fashion show in Milan last week, model Gigi Hadid obligingly smiled and posed for selfies with a crowd of fans. Suddenly, without warning, a man approached Hadid from behind and grabbed her, physically lifting her off her feet and into the air. Hadid swung her elbow backwards, forcing the man to release her and run away.

It must have been a terrifying moment. But instead of focusing on Hadid's well-being or praising her for her quick instincts, the international media had another angle in mind. 'NOT MODEL BEHAVIOUR' blared one disapproving headline. Another said 'Furious supermodel ... lashes out', emphasizing that she had to be 'held back by security', as if she had reacted with undue aggression. While some publications came to her defence, the general consensus was that a highly strung and violent Hadid had overreacted. When *Marie Claire* ran an article praising Hadid for her actions, the magazine's Twitter account shared it with the tagline 'unpopular opinion'. Multiple media outlets suggested that the perpetrator, Vitalii Sediuk, was a 'fan' of Hadid's, subtly implying that she owed him some debt of gratitude.

He is in fact a repeat offender who deliberately targets celebrities. Before the story had died down, Sediuk struck again, this time ambushing Kim Kardashian as she entered a restaurant in Paris. Sediuk lunged at Kardashian, attempting to grab her leg and kiss her bottom, before being pulled to the floor by a security guard. Yet again, the media responded bafflingly. BBC *Newsbeat* chose to turn the issue into a 'debate', tweeting: 'Is it OK to grab a woman on the street, even if it's for a "prank"?' The linked article presents the issue as a dilemma, giving space to Sediuk's excuses and 'explanations', including his claim that he was 'protesting Kim for using fake butt implants'. Other outlets have also described Sediuk's actions as a form of protest, and described them as pranks and stunts.

These aren't jokes, they are scary and unacceptable attacks. It isn't a coincidence that many of them deliberately target women, nor that the 'pranks' are often of a sexual nature and in several cases would clearly constitute a form of assault. In another example, Sediuk famously ambushed actor America Ferrera, trying to crawl underneath her dress on the red carpet at Cannes. This time, he was described in media reports as a 'pest' and 'unwanted guest'.

While the media reaction must be upsetting for the individuals involved (Hadid herself responded by pointing out that she had every right to defend herself), it also has a trickle-down effect for the rest of us. Such attitudes under-line the message that women should be gracious and grateful for any male attention, even when it takes an aggressive and unwanted form. They cast men who approach and manhan-dle women in the street as cheeky chappies and women who object as angry harpies. In short, they only exacerbate the street harassment thousands of women already face on a daily basis. Whether it's on the red carpet or the pavement, it's time we started to recognize these assaults for what they really are.

Originally published 1 October 2016

LESLIE JONES'S TWITTER ABUSE PROVES RELYING ON USERS TO REPORT BULLIES ISN'T ENOUGH

Breitbart technology editor Milo Yiannopoulos has been permanently banned from Twitter for breaking its rules against 'participating in or inciting targeted abuse of individuals', after he was said to have fanned the flames of sickening abuse directed at *Ghostbusters* actor Leslie Jones.

Jones quit the platform after a torrent of tweets, from messages comparing her to apes and videos of people screaming racist epithets, to people sending her images of her face covered in semen. On Tuesday evening, she wrote: 'I leave Twitter tonight with tears and a very sad heart. All this cause I did a movie. You can hate the movie but the shit I got today . . . wrong'.

She hasn't tweeted since.

In response, Yiannopoulos told Breitbart: 'With the cowardly suspension of my account, Twitter has confirmed itself as a safe space for Muslim terrorists and Black Lives Matter extremists, but a no-go zone for conservatives. This is the end for Twitter. Anyone who cares about free speech has been sent a clear message: you're not welcome on Twitter.'

Of course, this is nonsense. Freedom of speech doesn't include the freedom to abuse or incite racial hatred. And in such tantrums about the right to offend – tantamount to a bully throwing his toys out of the pram – we hear nothing about the silenced free speech of those who, like Jones, are driven off social media platforms because the sheer level of vitriol is just too much to bear.

If Twitter takes effective action against racist and misogynistic bullies, this has the potential to be the beginning, not the end. The beginning of the platform as a space that is open to all to express and debate views, instead of a hate-filled pit where members of minority groups are threatened, abused and taunted.

But banning one high-profile user is nowhere near enough to achieve that reality. The abuse being hurled at Jones has starkly highlighted the fact that despite years of paying lip service to the problem, Twitter and other social media platforms have utterly failed their users over tackling abuse.

On Monday night, Twitter released a statement: 'This type of abusive behavior is not permitted on Twitter, and we've taken action on many of the accounts reported to us by both Leslie and others. We rely on people to report this type of behavior to us but we are continuing to invest heavily in improving our tools and enforcement systems to prevent this kind of abuse. We realize we still have a lot of work in front of us before Twitter is where it should be on how we handle these issues.'

But what became very clear in Jones's case was that relying on people to report this type of behaviour is completely inadequate in cases where a storm of co-ordinated abuse has been stirred up and deliberately incited against an individual. This is a scenario many women, and in particular women of colour, disabled people and members of the LGBTQIA community will recognize only too well.

These incidents of co-ordinated abuse are often instigated

by influential users with thousands of followers, or even planned on a separate website or forum, where the victim is singled out as a target in advance. In these cases, it should be possible for a user simply to report the situation to Twitter. Moderators should monitor the situation and tackle the abusers as a group. There should be no need for the victim to trawl through and report accounts individually. Moderators could easily review each tweet using a particular user's handle over the past twenty-four hours.

This wouldn't require any alteration of Twitter's community guidelines on what is and isn't acceptable, simply more proactive implementation. This more victim-centred approach seems so mind-blowingly obvious that the fact it doesn't seem to have been tried before makes Twitter's claim to be working hard on this issue hard to swallow.

As Ijeoma Oluo points out, the impact of this problem reaches way beyond social media. By effectively denying women of colour access to these spaces, it not only removes their freedom of speech, but also access to vital professional networks, visibility, fan interaction and promotion of their work.

The abuse against Jones comes in the same week that Facebook's global head of safety admitted the platform is failing to meet its own standards on dealing with rape threats and abuse. And just last year, Twitter's chief executive acknowledged that the company 'sucks at dealing with abuse and trolls on the platform, and we've sucked at it for years'. Against this backdrop, with companies openly conceding that they are failing to protect users, the idea that it's really bullies such as Yiannopoulos who are being persecuted is laughable.

He claims that his banning signals the end of Twitter, but what might actually bring the platform down is its ongoing failure to tackle online bullying. The success of social media platforms relies entirely upon us, their users. If they can't take measurable, decisive action to tackle the kind of sickening abuse Jones and others receive, they no longer deserve our membership or support.

Originally published 21 July 2016

WOMEN ARE PEOPLE, TOO

In August 2016, a 64-year-old American woman named Darlene Horton was stabbed to death in Russell Square. Two days later, the BBC news homepage featured the headline: 'US woman killed in London attack named'. The subheading read: 'The US citizen killed in a knife attack in Russell Square, central London, is named as an eminent university professor's wife.' In June 2017, Page Six ran the headline: 'T. J. Miller's wife making a name for herself in New York' – prompting tweeter Ari Fishbein to comment drily, 'I've never seen a one-sentence headline contradict itself.' When acclaimed fashion designer L'Wren Scott died in 2014, headlines on her passing ranged from 'Mick Jagger's girlfriend found dead' to 'Rolling Stones cancel Perth concert'.

Again and again, in life and even in death, women are defined, if at all, by their relationship to men. The impact ranges from the underestimation of female achievement to far more serious consequences. Medicine provides us with one clear example. New drugs are predominantly tested on male subjects, and their development is based on the needs of the male body. There is growing evidence to suggest that for decades women have been taking the wrong doses and experiencing more adverse side effects to many medications than their male peers. It was not until 2013, for example, that scientists realized women's bodies metabolized certain sleeping pills far more slowly than men, resulting in a dramatic reduction of the dosage instructions for women.

Astonishingly, it was also not until 2013 that Swedish researchers created the world's first female crash test dummy, meaning that all previous car designs had been based on best protecting the male form from injury. Tests suggested this left women at greater risk of harm from injuries such as whiplash.

Then there are women who experience still greater 'othering', from Muslim women whose veils seem to preclude some from seeing them as humans, to feminists who are painted as monstrous caricatures, to BAME women who face racist abuse intertwined and enmeshed with misogyny. There are women forgotten and allowed to fall between the cracks, from female prisoners to those with special needs facing issues such as forced marriage. And there are situations in which 'female' still seems to be seen as a special category, where men once again form the default and those few women who are included are supposed to be grateful for being mentioned at all.

Experiments that ask groups of children to draw doctors, astronauts, police officers, lawyers and any other number of professionals reveal that they automatically draw male figures. Again and again, our immediate assumption that 'human' means 'male' leaves women at best an afterthought, at worst erased, disadvantaged or endangered.

'NORMAL' IN OUR SOCIETY
MEANS MALE – WOMEN ARE
WRITTEN OUT OF THE STORY

It has famously been said that feminism is the radical notion that women are people. While this distinction may seem obvious, it remains a confusing area for some – not least sports reporter John Inverdale. Congratulating Andy Murray on his second tennis Olympic gold medal, Inverdale told him: 'You're the first person ever to win two Olympic tennis gold medals', leaving Murray to point out that 'Venus and Serena [Williams] have won about four each.'

Just days earlier, while commenting on the men's rugby sevens event, Inverdale reportedly announced that the winning team would be taking home the first-ever Olympic medal for the sport, despite the women's title having already been claimed by Australia less than a week before. All this has led to the mystery of the week, the question on everybody's lips: has Inverdale forgotten that women exist, or does he just not realize that they are people? In fairness to Inverdale, he is far from alone. Women have a pesky habit of slipping minds at important moments – just ask those reporters who discussed our hypothetical new prime minister using 'he' and 'him' before being left red-faced by Theresa May's victory.

It's not surprising that Murray picked up on the error – it's only three years since he was lavishly congratulated on the front pages for ending the '77-year wait' for a British Wimbledon champion. Which is true. As long as you don't consider Virginia Wade, who won Wimbledon in 1977, and three previous female winners since Fred Perry's 1936 victory, to be people.

It is telling that we are so used to such omissions that Murray's simple statement of fact about the Williams sisters has received rapturous applause across the media and the internet. Under the circumstances, it is remarkable and hugely welcome to see a man in his position be so thoughtful as to acknowledge women's existence. But wouldn't it be nice if it was the norm rather than the exception?

The problem isn't confined to sport either. When Tim Peake was hailed in the media as the first Briton to blast off into space last December, it must have come as a surprise to Helen Sharman, who beat him to it by more than twenty years.

So ingrained is our society's default male norm, in fact, that many media outlets choose to point out that people are female in newspaper headlines, as if the idea they aren't male is as newsworthy as the event they were involved in: 'Hero gas station clerk saves female doctor from suspected kidnapper'; 'Female judge Constance Briscoe investigated over leaking Chris Huhne case, court told'; 'Female Belgian rower falls ill after racing on Guanabara bay'; 'Woman cyclist fighting for life after horrific crash at danger junction'.

The same shock manifests itself when subjects deviate from other expected norms, too, as swimmer Simone Manuel discovered when her gold medal victory was reduced in headlines to: 'Michael Phelps shares historic night with African-American'. The implication is that white men are individuals – human beings in their own right, with personalities and quirks and rich, rounded lives – while other people are still defined as members of homogenous 'othered' groups.

This matters beyond the technicality of who gets named in a headline. It impacts on how sympathetic our society is likely to be towards those described. It contributes to the stereotyping and vilification of entire groups who are tarred, sweepingly, with a single brush. It writes out of history those whose contributions we most need to highlight in order to rectify inequality in sport, science and other fields.

Leaving women out of the story isn't a simple slip-up. It is a consequence of a world that tells us they just aren't quite as important. That their achievements don't really count. It means that even now, some of us do still need reminding that women are people, too.

Originally published 17 August 2016

DAVID CAMERON WILL SUPPORT MUSLIM WOMEN – BUT ONLY WHEN IT SUITS HIS SCAREMONGERING NARRATIVE

David Cameron this week announced a £20m language fund particularly targeted at British Muslim women. The prime minister claimed that some 190,000 British Muslim women, or 22 per cent, speak little or no English, and suggested that a minority of men were promoting 'backward attitudes' and exerting 'damaging control' over their female relatives.

But while Cameron's commitment to funding for English language classes was welcomed in many quarters (particularly in light of previous £45m cuts to the ESOL budget), he also drew unnecessary and unclear links between the English language skills of Muslim women and extremism, as well as appearing to threaten that migrants who failed to reach a particular standard of English may not be allowed to remain in the UK.

The conflation of these very different issues seemed to suggest that the rights and empowerment of Muslim women are only of particular concern when they are instrumental in protecting the rest of Britain from the threat of extremism, not to mention simultaneously casting Muslim women as suppressed victims and dangerous outsiders. Of course, measures to tackle oppression and violence against women should be applauded – and Cameron did make a point of stating that these are not issues confined to Muslim communities – but this was undermined by his singling out of Muslim women in particular, as many pointed out.

On Twitter, Baroness Sayeeda Warsi – former minister of state for faith and communities – said: 'Women should have the opportunity to learn English full stop. Why link it to radicalization/extremism?' She added: 'And why should it just be Muslim women who have the opportunity to learn English? Why not anyone who lives in the UK and can't speak English?' She also highlighted the problem of a blanket suggestion that mothers who don't speak English well might raise children who are integrated less or who are less likely to contribute positively to society, saying: 'PS mums English isn't great yet she inspired her girls to become a Lawyer, teacher, accountant, pharmacist, cabinet minister #WomenPower' [sic].

A statement from the Bradford-based Muslim Women's Council read: 'Whilst we welcome the additional funding pledged today by the prime minister for English language support for Muslim women, we do not agree with the assertion that there is a link between a lack of English and extremism. David Cameron is conflating these two issues and is further isolating the very same group of people that he is trying to reach and assist.'

Although the language funding has been generally greeted as a step in the right direction, it will do little to protect Muslim women from the hate crime that has spiked by more than 300 per cent since the Paris terror attacks, with women and girls as the majority of victims. Nor will it offset the Islamophobia that saw the winner of *The Great British Bake Off*, Nadiya Hussain, worry she had 'put her kids in danger' by appearing on the show, or address instances like that of the 10-year-old Muslim boy questioned by police apparently because he made a spelling mistake and wrote that he lived in a 'terrorist' rather than a 'terraced' house. Nor does it alleviate the inherent bias that plays a role in the economic inactivity to which Cameron referred among women of Pakistani and Bangladeshi heritage, who often face discrimination when seeking employment. Nor does it resolve the funding crisis that currently leaves 67 per cent of BAME women's specialist support services uncertain of their future.

And while, of course, it is right to tackle instances of gender discrimination within British Muslim communities (a fight long led by Muslim women themselves), it is short-sighted to imply that this is the only direction from which women in the UK, Muslim or otherwise, are likely to experience sexism, discrimination, violence and abuse.

It is important for the prime minister to declare with such zeal that he wants to tackle the 'minority of men' who perpetuate misogynistic attitudes and 'exert damaging control' – but the same determination should apply to those exerting dominance and control over the one in four women in England and Wales who experience domestic violence.

Of course we should be offering language classes, and other forms of support, to anybody in the UK who needs it. But it isn't enough to give with one hand and take away with another, or to extend support to Muslim women only when it suits a scaremongering narrative.

Originally published 21 January 2016

WHERE ARE ALL THE WOMEN, WIKIPEDIA?

It is often said that women have been written out of history. We have all heard of Alexander Graham Bell and Thomas Edison, but few are familiar with their contemporary, Margaret E. Knight, a prolific American inventor who held over twenty patents and was decorated by Queen Victoria. Knight created her first device, a safety mechanism for textile machines, after witnessing a factory accident aged just twelve. She later invented a machine that created the flat-bottomed paper bags still used in grocery stores today. When she died in 1914, an obituary described her as a 'woman Edison'. Somewhat dispiritingly, she has also been described as 'the most famous nineteenth-century woman inventor'. But how many of us know her name?

If you were to try and research Knight's life and work, you might struggle. Her Wikipedia profile is just under 500 words long; Edison's is more than 8,500. Of course, Edison's contribution to the development of the electric light warrants a significant write-up, and his legacy deserves a lengthy profile. But his Wikipedia page also contains minute detail about his early life, diets and views on religion. By contrast, information on Knight's page is scant, though she too invented an item still widely used today. Her profile lacks many details (including any mention of her first invention), which are available elsewhere online, particularly on websites dedicated to commemorating the work of female inventors. That such resources exist says a lot about the erasure of women such as Knight from more mainstream information sources.

This week, it was revealed that only around 17 per cent of notable profiles on Wikipedia are of women. While we bemoan the sexist bias that prevented many historic female figures from being rightly commemorated and celebrated, there is a risk that history may be repeating itself all over again.

Perhaps the disparity is unsurprising given that only around 15 per cent of Wikipedia's volunteer editors are female. Reasons suggested for the gender gap have ranged from the elitist nature of the 'hard-driving hacker crowd' to the overt harassment and misogyny faced by female editors on the site. When one editor suggested a women-only space on Wikipedia for female contributors to support one another and discuss online misogyny, other users vowed to fight the proposal 'to the death'.

The trouble with Wikipedia having such a vast gender gap in its notable profiles is that it is one of the most commonly used information sources in the world. A 2011 study found that 53 per cent of all American internet users look for information on Wikipedia, increasing to almost 70 per cent of college-educated users. According to web-traffic data company Alexa, it is currently the fifth most visited website in the world. For such a popular source to present millions of students, researchers and journalists with a hugely gender-biased roster of articles could have a real impact on everything, from young people's career aspirations to which high-profile figures are invited to speak at conferences and events.

There are ongoing efforts to solve the problem, such as this week's BBC 100 Women edit-a-thon, which will see fifteen events in thirteen countries happening in multiple languages to grow the number of female editors and to add profiles for women who deserve to be recognized. Meanwhile, Wikipedia founder Jimmy Wales has called for a more inclusive and diverse community of editors. Wales himself has pointed out that the process by which Wikipedia editors decide collectively whether a particular topic deserves its own article could lead to biased outcomes when those editors are overwhelmingly male. Various projects have been launched to try and address the problem, but progress seems slow.

Knight probably wouldn't have been surprised by the disparity. In her own lifetime, she faced sexism and discrimination from men – in particular from Charles Annan, who spied on her paper-bag-production prototype and tried to steal the patent, even arguing in court that a woman could never have invented such an innovative machine. But she might have imagined that the gender gap would have improved rather more significantly by now.

Originally published 9 December 2016

FORCED MARRIAGE IS STILL
A BIG PROBLEM IN THE UK.
WHAT MORE CAN WE DO?

This month, a 34-year-old businessman from Cardiff became the first person in the UK to be jailed under the forced-marriage laws introduced in June 2014. Forced marriage is defined as when one or both spouses do not consent to the marriage, or when consent is extracted under duress – which can include physical, psychological, financial, sexual and emotional pressure. Iwan Jenkins, head of the Crown Prosecution Service's rape and serious sexual offences unit in Wales, said: 'Forced marriage wrecks lives and destroys families. We hope that today's sentence sends a strong message that forced marriage will not be tolerated in today's Britain.'

According to the Home Office, in 2014 the Forced Marriage Unit – set up in 2005 to promote and enforce the government's policy on the issue – gave advice or support to 1,267 cases, 79 per cent of which involved female victims. Over 10 per cent involved victims with disabilities and 11 per cent of cases involved victims under the age of sixteen.

Progress on addressing the issue is slow, and campaigners and academics have raised questions about the efficacy of the new laws, given that only one conviction has taken place in the year since they came into effect. Respond, a UK-based charity supporting people with learning disabilities affected by trauma and abuse, this month launched My Life, My Marriage, a project aimed at challenging the practice of forcing marriage on people with learning disabilities. The project will seek to raise awareness about the problem, and will offer advocacy to people with learning disabilities and their support networks, and training to professionals, practitioners and community leaders. It will include an educational roadshow and sessions in schools to educate young people with learning disabilities about forced marriage.

Luthfa Khan, who is leading the project, explained that the campaign came about in response to a number of cases Respond has dealt with over the years involving possible forced marriages. At the launch of the project in London last week, Khan suggested that the number of cases dealt with by the Home Office is likely to be 'just touching the surface'. Highlighting the complexity of the problem, she cautioned that the cases that Respond deals with are nuanced and varied, and may look very different from people's conception of forced marriage.

The issue of consent is one of those complexities. While Respond is supportive of people with learning disabilities who are able to give consent and do make the decision to get married freely, Khan is keen to stress the importance of providing support for those who may be pressured into doing so: 'Through our referral service, we aim to work towards removing labels which further victimize people, taking each case on its own merit and working with people to fully understand what is actually happening within each situation.'

She explains how nuanced some of the cases can be: 'Within many families, there can be a belief that marriage is a rite of passage and some families may even perhaps wish or hope that it will "cure" the person of learning disabilities. Other families, particularly where there are older parents, might be worried about who will look after their son or daughter after they are gone. So through marriage they are hoping to bring in someone who will be a lifetime carer. Even if carried out benignly, they have not considered that the person with learning disabilities once married will have to deal with [issues like] sex, having children, a commitment to another person and compromises when living with someone else. And worse than this, they may face rejection once the spouse realizes that they have a disability or even worse they may be physically, emotionally and/or sexually abused. But also, increasingly, we are seeing people with learning disabilities becoming targeted for forced marriage through coercion or trickery in order to extract their finances or accommodation or even for passports or visas.'

Respond chief executive Noelle Blackman worries that the nuance of the cases they see is not allowed for by the new legislation: 'The new Health and [Social] Care Act promotes advocacy for people with learning disabilities, but we are concerned that this is likely to come from generic advocacy agencies without the specialized knowledge that would be needed.'

Let's hope, as Khan does, that this first case to be prosecuted 'will send out a very strong message'. And, as slow progress continues to be made towards addressing the problem of forced marriage, My Life, My Marriage will continue to highlight the complexity of the issue, supporting victims who might otherwise fall through the gaps.

Originally published 26 June 2015

BABIES BEHIND BARS: WHY
CAMERON'S SUPPORT OF PRISON
REFORM FALLS SHORT

On Monday, David Cameron made a speech about the need for comprehensive prison reform, including a particular mention of the detention of pregnant women and mothers with young babies. Speaking at the Policy Exchange think tank in Westminster, he said: 'A sad but true fact is that last year there were 100 babies in our country living in a prison. Yes, actually inside the prison. In the prison's mother-and-baby unit, to be precise. When we know the importance of the early years for child development, how can we possibly justify having babies behind bars?'

Under the new reforms, the government would consider alternative forms of dealing with offenders, including satellite-tagging technology and 'problem-solving courts', which would order offenders into treatment programmes for issues such as drug addiction.

Cameron was right to raise the issue of the catastrophic state of the prison system (he's the first prime minister for twenty years to do so, in a speech solely focusing on prisons), and right to recommend reform. The current system is not working, as the statistics show: 46 per cent of all prisoners and 60 per cent of those with short sentences reoffend within a year. The situation is equally dire for prisoners' well-being: there are, on average, 600 incidents of self-harm in prisons every week. But the problem demands a more comprehensive solution than Cameron suggests, particularly with regard to women.

More than 9,000 women were received into prison last year, the majority for non-violent offences. An estimated 17,240 children, including many under five years old, are separated from their mothers by imprisonment. Only 5 per cent of children with a mother in prison are able to stay in the family home, and only 9 per cent are cared for by their fathers. In 2011–12, according to the Prison Reform Trust, just 8.7 per cent of women were able to find employment on release, compared with 27.3 per cent of men.

According to the London-based charity Women in Prison, 46 per cent of women in prison report having suffered domestic violence, and 53 per cent report having experienced emotional, physical or sexual abuse during childhood (compared with 27 per cent of men). Despite making up only 5 per cent of the prison population, women in prison account for 28 per cent of the self-harm incidents. Women in custody are five times more likely to have a mental health concern than women in the general population and 46 per cent say they have attempted suicide at some time in their life. Many vulnerable women end up in prison because they have been coerced into committing crimes by male partners or family members; in 2013, 48 per cent of women said they committed their crime in order to support the drug habit of someone else.

The problem doesn't end when women enter prison – former inmates have described abuse, and a recent report by national charity the Howard League for Penal Reform found that female prisoners had been coerced into sex and pressured into abusive relationships with staff.

It is already clear that sustainable, properly funded alternatives to custody are a vital part of making any prison-reform plan work. This is especially true for prisoners with complex needs, including those who have experienced domestic or sexual abuse, and single mothers. But this is where Cameron's passionate support of reform could fall short in the light of funding cuts to specialist services for supporting female offenders and cuts to domestic and sexual violence services.

There is evidence that the financial cost of such services would be negligible. According to the Prison Reform Trust, if alternatives to prison were to achieve an additional reduction of just 6 per cent in reoffending by women, the state would recoup the investment required in just one year.

If we want to resolve the gargantuan problem of the failing prison service, a wider view needs to be taken and it must include real, well-funded action on violence against women; not only responsive measures, but preventative ones, too. It is also vital to take into account the experiences of all women. The charity Women for Refugee Women has been campaigning against the detention of refugee women, including those who are pregnant, for some time.

Natasha Walter, director of the charity, says: 'Detaining pregnant women is ineffective: in 2014, 99 pregnant women were held in Yarl's Wood detention centre – despite government policy that these women should only be detained in exceptional circumstances – but only nine of these women were actually removed from the UK. Ninety per cent were released to continue with their cases in the community, so their detention served no purpose at all. In January 2016, a review of the welfare of vulnerable detainees, commissioned by the Home Office and undertaken by the former prisons and probation ombudsman Stephen Shaw, recommended that there should be an absolute ban on the use of immigration detention for pregnant women.

Urgent attention is also due to the plight of transgender women serving sentences in UK prisons, an issue not raised in Cameron's speech; particularly after the tragic deaths of Joanne Latham and Vicky Thompson within a single month in 2015. A review of the care and management of transgender offenders is currently underway.

These issues affect some of the most voiceless members of our society. Cameron should be commended for broaching the subject of prison reform. But for female prisoners in particular, there is a lot more that needs to be said.

Originally published 11 February 2016

WOMEN'S SUPPORT SERVICES SAVE LIVES. SO WHY IS THE GOVERNMENT CUTTING THEIR FUNDING?

A powerful new report from the black feminist organization Imkaan has revealed a state of emergency among black and minority ethnic (BME) women's groups working to end violence against women and girls and providing specialist support for survivors. The report, which campaigners handed in to Downing Street along with a petition to protect such services, outlines a funding crisis affecting BME services, including refuges, helplines, outreach and advice provision.

In this week's spending review, Chancellor George Osborne announced that, instead of ending the 'tampon tax' (which requires women to pay 5 per cent VAT on sanitary items by classing them as a luxury), he would use the £15m levied by the tax to help fund women's charities. But quite apart from the problematic conflation of periods and refuges which, intentionally or not, suggests male violence against women is a women's problem for women to solve, his speech didn't make clear how the funding would be distributed or whether charities, apart from those explicitly named, would be supported. Even a major national organization, such as Rape Crisis, which wasn't named in the Chancellor's speech, remains uncertain of its future, with a spokesperson saying the charity is in 'a very precarious position'. For smaller, specialist organizations, which are more likely to get their funding from local councils, deep cuts to local government budgets mean that the situation remains hazardous.

Responding to the spending review, the End Violence Against Women Coalition pointed out the 'alarming 29 per cent cut to the Communities Department budget' and expressed serious concern about the impact this could have on violence against women specialist support services. It concluded: 'Today's announcement fails to offer them a life raft.'

There are more than thirty-four dedicated specialist BME violence against women and girls services in the UK, offering flexible and diverse support systems that take into account the specific and complex needs of their service users. But when Imkaan, which acts as an umbrella group for BME organizations, surveyed its members, a shocking 67 per cent reported uncertainty about their sustainability in the current climate. One organization responded: 'Very uncertain. We did a tender for a refuge in April/ May and still don't know the outcome. If it is not given to us, it will mean we close in the next year or so.'

Imkaan's report finds that BME women and children in the UK have great and urgent need of specialist services, which uniquely understand the situations they face. During the last financial year, in London alone, 733 BME women sought refuge spaces and only 154 were successful. Nationally, seventeen BME violence against women and girls organizations supported a total of 21,713 women, also over the course of just one year.

Marai Larasi MBE, executive director of Imkaan, says: 'These organizations are well known in the communities they serve and have the highest numbers of women approaching them directly, rather than being referred on by police, social workers or others. Bigger, more generic services are rarely able to achieve this profile or these "self-referrals". If these services are lost, lives will be lost. When this lesson is learned, it will be hard to start again and rebuild. We urge the government to show that it understands the needs of BME women facing violence and to commit to a nationally ring-fenced funding solution.'

As funding cuts continue to impact the women's sector, the report highlights a trend towards councils awarding funding to larger generic providers at the cost of specialized services. Apna Haq, Rotherham's only BME women's service, remains at risk of closure after its £145,000 contract for providing domestic violence support was terminated by the council in favour of a mainstream provider with no specialism in minority ethnic women's needs, which could carry out the work at a slightly lower price.

Zlakha Ahmed, executive director of Apna Haq, says: 'Independent, specialist and dedicated services, run by and for the communities we seek to serve, are life-saving. Our "led by and for" services offer uniquely empowering experiences to women and children as service users are reflected in staffing, management and governance structures ... Demand is increasing every day. We, and many others, simply cannot afford to close.'

In 2012, the European Institute for Gender Equality carried out a review of the implementation of the Beijing Platform for Action in the EU member states on violence against women and victim support. One finding of that review reads: 'Specialist BME services are in short supply throughout the European Union. As a result, it is of upmost importance for member states to strive to support their existence, in order to not only provide effective support for BME women and children, but also to contribute to states' fulfilment of their human rights obligations in the area of combating violence against women, including Article 22 of provision of specialist support services, as specified in the Council of Europe Convention on preventing and combating violence against women and domestic violence.'

The convention referred to, also known as the Istanbul Convention, came into force twelve months ago. It specifies the requirement for short- and long-term specialist services for those who have experienced violence against women. But despite signing up to it three years ago, the UK government has still failed to ratify it. In February this year, the Joint Committee on Human Rights released a report under the headline 'Government doing less at home than abroad on violence against women and girls', in which it explicitly warned that the government could harm its international reputation by failing to ratify the convention. And in March, Women's Aid received a letter from David Cameron confirming that the coalition government would not ratify the Istanbul Convention, allowing the issue to drag on. Though eighteen states, including Italy, France, Spain, Denmark and Sweden have all ratified the convention, the UK still has yet to do so.

Ratification would mean that the UK government would have to bring its provision, such as the one cited above relating to specialist support services, into force through domestic policy and legislation. While it drags its feet, services providing specialist provision for black and minority ethnic women are at crisis point.

Originally published 30 November 2015

SEXISM, DOUBLE DISCRIMINATION AND MORE THAN ONE KIND OF PREJUDICE

Since the Everyday Sexism Project started, many of the stories we have catalogued have described not just sexism, but sexism intermingled with other forms of prejudice – racism, homophobia, transphobia, classism, ageism, disableism, stigma around mental health problems, and more. Again and again, we've heard from women in same-sex relationships being fetishized and asked for threesomes when they're just trying to walk down the street, trans women mocked and belittled and hounded from public spaces, Asian women being labelled as 'easy' or 'obedient', sex workers accused of being complicit in their own assaults, disabled women infantilized and patronized, and countless similar stories.

'Double discrimination' (or, indeed, triple or quadruple) has proved to be a major recurring theme within the project and is a crucial focus for modern feminism. Intersectionality means being aware of and acting on the fact that different forms of prejudice are connected, because they all stem from the same root of being other, different or somehow secondary to the 'normal', 'ideal' status quo. So just as women suffer from sexism because our society is set up to favour and automatically take men as the norm from which women deviate, so the same is true for people who are different from other dominant norms – such as being heterosexual, white, cisgendered and non-disabled. People also often face prejudice as a result of other characteristics, such as age, class and religious belief.

If we are to tackle the fact that women have been

historically oppressed because of characteristics that are seen to be different from the male norm, how can we protest such treatment while simultaneously excluding from our own movement the needs and agendas of those with other stigmatized characteristics? This is particularly true in the case of our trans sisters, who some feminists believe should be excluded from some areas of the movement by virtue of not fulfilling required characteristics of womanhood – a deep irony for a group fighting for equality regardless of sex.

There were huge numbers of project entries that clearly demonstrate two or more kinds of prejudice combined. Many women of colour, for example, have described suffering not only from both racism and sexism but also from a particular brand of racist sexism that conflates and exacerbates the two.

'I am Japanese. Frequently told by white men that Japanese, Chinese, Filipina, Asian women are "better" than the "feminazis", "femicunts" in the West and "know how to treat men"; we will cook and clean.'

'I was walking on my university campus with my boyfriend, when we walked past a group of guys, one of whom shouted out "What did you pay for her then? Is she a mail order?" My boyfriend is Chinese and I'm half Indian.'

Writer Reni Eddo-Lodge says that not all women experience incidents like street harassment in the same way: 'There's particular fascination with African women's bodies and because of the likes of hip-hop videos – the production of which is controlled by black men in a heavily male-dominated industry – our bodies are rarely equated with innocence and piety and instead are deemed as permanently sexually available.' This idea of black women as exotic, hyper-sexualized creatures can be seen again and again in cultural stereotypes. Try typing 'pretty' into Google image search and you are greeted with pages and pages of white women's faces (the fashion industry is notoriously white: of the seventy-five British *Vogue* covers since the beginning of 2008, black women have featured on just three, while Kate Moss alone has graced nine); but type in 'sexy' and suddenly far more women of colour appear – though they remain far less represented than white women. Sexism impacts hugely on women's lives, careers and success. When prejudices intersect, the same is doubly true.

And, as demonstrated by accounts of other forms of sexism, these combined prejudices become evident at a tragically young age. 'I reported a boy at school who had been making racial and sexual remarks to me and other girls of ethnic minorities for about a year. Because, even though teachers and other students could hear the disgusting comments he was making about me being a "black whore who he wanted to put in a cage", a Pakistani girl being a "bomber" and stating the only attractive females were white, it was dismissed and nobody said a word.'

The huge effect of media stereotypes on the treatment of particular groups of people – especially those suffering various forms of double discrimination – is a vital part of the problem. According to new figures released in May 2013, just 18 per cent of television presenters over the age of fifty are women. The percentage for disabled women, LGBTQIA women and women of colour is likely to be even lower.

The problem is exacerbated and inflamed by two key factors. First, such women are so rarely portrayed on screen as to be considered strange and unusual. Second, when they are present they have generally been moulded into hackneyed caricatures that play to every stereotype in the book and exist solely to satisfy a specific storyline.

'The dearth of any women in the media anywhere near my size (I'm a UK 18) who isn't a) a pathetic lonely loser or b) the "before" shot on a weight-loss show.'

'As a physically disabled woman, I feel invisible, both in the media and in real life. No one seems to think that I have a sexuality or even sensuality. There seem to be very few characters in films and TV shows who are incidentally disabled and/or queer.'

'Next to no programmes portray lesbians as just one of the double-discrimination characters, without being a story feature and portrayed to meet (hetero male?) viewer expectations. I'd note that we are a diverse bunch and don't have a "look" so much!'

'The media's complete failure to be able to cover trans folk in any way that considers them as people first and trans second – instead, it is always made to be their entire identity, whether in the rare television shows when a trans person features or in the papers, where they insist on referring to people like Chelsea Manning as "Bradley" and "he" irrespective of her own wishes.'

'Working-class women are rarely portrayed in a good light in the media, and equality of opportunity rather than focusing on women at the top is something feminism needs more of.'

The battle can feel endless – because it is a far more complex issue than just achieving representation in itself. Before trans people can even begin to fight for equality, for instance, they first have to overcome enormous ignorance and lack of understanding about their experience.

'A close friend of mine is a trans man and has been told many times by people who knew him before his transition (which began towards the end of his time at high school) or have seen pictures of him as a child that "it's a shame such a pretty girl wants to look like a guy", implying that his gender identity is a choice and deliberately neglecting the duty of anyone born with female organs to look feminine.'

One of the reasons why it is so important to let members of oppressed groups tell their own stories in their own ways is that it's so easy to think you're getting it when you're not. In much the same way as many of the men writing to the project said they thought they knew about sexism when they imagined a catcall or a wolf whistle but had no concept of how it actually impacted on women's lives, living it every day, influencing every choice and thought. Because it isn't just about the individual incidents; it's about the collective impact on everything else – the way you think about yourself, the way you approach public spaces and human interaction, the limits you place on your own aspirations and the things you stop yourself from doing before you even try because of bitter learned experience.

As the writer John Scalzi brilliantly and simply put it on his blog, Whatever: 'In the role-playing game known as The Real World, "Straight White Male" is the lowest difficulty setting there is.' Of course, this is not to discount the difficulties faced by, for example, heterosexual white men from disadvantaged socioeconomic backgrounds but it's a ballpark starting point that helps us get the general idea.

This sense of instantly being judged and condemned purely as a result of others' preconceptions also comes across painfully clearly in the entries we have received from disabled women.

'Strangers saying: "You're hot . . . for a girl in a wheelchair."'

'I was once assaulted by an older man twice my size getting onto a bus because he thought I looked too young to be using a walking stick so I had to be a "scrounging lazy little bitch".'

Feminists need to include these varied priorities and experiences within the movement for equality. As blogger Dee Emm Elms, who writes Four-Color Princesses, says: 'That person on the bus being harassed is still being harassed whether he's being harassed for being religious or for being an atheist or being black or being a woman or because of her clothing or because of her body language or because of her appearance or because of her handbag or because of her accent. That's all the same problem. It's not recognizing the basic humanity of a person.'

Originally published 31 March 2014

Our Bodies, Our Battlegrounds

If I had to choose the most upsetting statistic I've ever come across, this one would come close to the top of the list: research shows that 80 per cent of 10-year-old American girls have dieted to lose weight.

Perhaps more than at any other time in history, women's bodies are burdened to breaking point with the weight of societal shame, pressure, judgement and exploitation. Girls are pushed to share Photoshopped photographs on social media, where images of celebrity ribcages, thigh gaps and cleavage abound. Young men are socialized to demand nude photographs to prove their 'lad' credentials, resulting in enormous pressure on girls to provide them, followed swiftly by censure and judgement, whether they comply (slut) or not (prude). Airbrushed adverts and magazine articles force endless unrealistic images of emaciated models upon us, without acknowledgement of the vast majority of women whose bodies don't look like those in the media spotlight. Those with bodies whose size, shape or skin colour aren't deemed 'beautiful' are variously shamed and mocked, or patronizingly praised as inspirational tokens, as if their mere existence is a form of bravery.

A billion-dollar industry works to undermine women's body confidence in order to sell them everything from spiralizers to cellulite zappers for invented problems they never knew they had. Vulvas and vaginas remain stigmatized, and the discussion of female sexual pleasure, and of conditions like endometriosis, period pain and thrush, is contained to hushed, shameful tones, while the international porn industry profits endlessly from the exposure and exploitation of those very same body parts.

Online porn teaches female viewers that their pubic hair is strange and unnatural and their ordinary labia ugly or lopsided, to the extent that leading gynaecologists have warned that enquiries about plastic surgery from girls as young as nine are fast increasing. In 2015–16, more than 200 girls under eighteen had labiaplasty on the NHS. It is the world's fastest-growing cosmetic procedure, with 45 per cent more operations carried out in 2016 than the preceding year. Pregnancy renders women's bodies automatic public property as they are subjected to a thousand high-pressure instructions about how to be pregnant, to birth, to breastfeed a baby, but simultaneously shamed for doing it the 'wrong' way or failing to instantly shed their 'baby weight'. Trans women face enormous pressure to conform to the bodily demands and curiosity of others, who see only genitalia and not humanity.

My friend and hero Emer O'Toole was invited on to a major breakfast television programme to 'debate' the fact that she'd chosen not to shave her armpits for a year, as if her personal bodily choices were a matter for public record and challenge. Which, of course, is exactly how women's bodies continue to be viewed – just ask our sisters who continue to battle for abortion rights after an Irish minor was placed in a psychiatric clinic against her will for requesting a termination and a Northern Irish woman who was forced to carry her baby for another fifteen weeks of pregnancy and go through a delivery despite having discovered at her twenty-week scan that the pregnancy was not viable.

From the ongoing scourge of female genital mutilation to the shaming of women with different body sizes and shapes, the hyper-sexualization of black women's bodies and the commodification of disembodied breasts and stomachs by advertising moguls, women's bodies remain tightly policed, debated and embattled. We are still dreaming of a world in which our bodies are our own business and nobody else's.

WHY IS WOMEN'S BODY IMAGE ANXIETY AT SUCH DEVASTATING LEVELS?

We need to talk about body image. New findings from the 2014 British Social Attitudes (BSA) survey reveal that only 63 per cent of women aged 18–34 and 57 per cent of women aged 35–49 are satisfied with their appearance.

In a world obsessed with women's bodies, we are bombarded with images of them, usually undressed, often dehumanized and reduced to parts and pieces, at every turn. But though we see women's bodies everywhere, it's only really one body that we're seeing, over and over again. Usually a young, thin, white, toned, large-breasted, long-legged, non-disabled body.

Funnily enough, that's not what most women's bodies look like. But the airbrushed media ideal is so powerful and so omnipresent that women find themselves comparing their own bodies to it anyway, and finding themselves wanting. The results are devastating. A recent report by the All Party Parliamentary Group on Body Image found that girls as young as five are worrying about their size and appearance, and that one in four 7-year-old girls has tried to lose weight at least once. And, as the BSA survey results show, a preoccupation with body image affects women throughout their lives, not just in their youth. It holds women back by eroding their confidence both at work and socially. New research coinciding with Body Confidence Week found that almost 10 million women in the UK 'feel depressed' because of the way they look and 36 per cent avoid exercise because of insecurity about their looks.

Unrealistic media ideals of female beauty have spawned a multitude of 'body confidence' campaigns, but many, like *The Sun*'s recently launched No More Skinny, only seem to want to shift us from coveting one ideal to another. Supported by male celebrities including singer Olly Murs and rapper Professor Green, an article about the campaign in the paper's Bizarre column quoted Murs lamenting, 'Gone are the days of Marilyn Monroe . . .' and later continuing, 'Sometimes skinny women can look attractive – but it is too dangerous.' By referencing Monroe, famously a sex symbol, and foregrounding the issue in women's attractiveness, the message once again seems to be about women adjusting their body shape to appeal to men's desire. Not to mention the fact that a curvaceous shape like Monroe's is just as unattainable for many women as a very thin physique. It misses the point entirely.

When you visit the latest column about 'No More Skinny' on *The Sun*'s website, the sidebar alongside the piece includes links to the following articles: 'Enter our *Sun* Lurves Curves comp to win £1K prize and modelling contract'; 'Lose 7 lb in seven days with *The Sun*'s new Back to School diet'; 'I shed 1 st 9 lb on *Sun* Slimmers diet . . . and you can too'; 'Bianca Gascoigne: "I lost a stone in six weeks on the No-Diet Diet"'.

Confused? I am. It's hardly 'empowering' to encourage women to eschew thinness in a media outlet presenting reams of methods offering to help them lose weight. (Nor, for that matter, one that publishes a regular picture of a young, slim woman topless on page 3). But the deeper point here is that trying to shift the ideal body shape shouldn't be the ultimate aim anyway – we need to stop judging people by their looks in the first place.

Worries about body image impact on both men and women – the BSA survey found that only three-quarters of men are satisfied with their appearance. But while it is true that we are all bombarded with idealistic images of bodies to aspire to, there is a marked difference in the scale and context of the problem. When the *Times Magazine* ran a picture of David Gandy in his underwear on the front cover last month, many people tweeted it to the Everyday Sexism Twitter account, presumably to point out that objectification is an issue that affects men, too. But the incident was the perfect example of the sort of context in which we tend to see these images of men's bodies – on an underwear model, in an article specifically about his new underwear range. Compare it to the multitude of front pages showing women, who are generally not models, partially or fully nude – in articles not related to underwear – while their male colleagues remain fully clothed. Or the coverage of female politicians' legs and fashion choices compared to men's voting records and credentials. Or a recent advert showing female founders and CEOs of tech companies in their underwear. Male equivalents? Not so much. To give another example, while men are portrayed as rounded, full characters in Hollywood films, women are often reduced to inconsequential sex objects. Research found that 32 per cent of female parts and over 50 per cent of teenage girl parts were sexualized in hit US films in 2012.

This insistence on valuing and judging women's bodies first and their careers or personalities second is insidious and powerful. In a world that holds up ridiculous and unrealistic standards as ideal, it means they are always doomed to fall short.

Telling us curvy is better, or patronizing us by suggesting we are our own worst body critics and should magically 'snap out of it', isn't going to help. Women will stop worrying about their looks when society stops telling us that they're all we're worth. Let's focus on that first.

Originally published 14 October 2014

IT'S TIME TO STOP BLAMING
WOMEN FOR HAVING BREASTS

Breasts are having a moment. Boobs, tits, baps, funbags – and all the other terms we come up with for a part of the anatomy society finds a little too dangerous to be comfortably called by its own name. (See also, vagina.) Whatever you want to call them, breasts have been firmly in the spotlight in recent weeks.

At a baptism ceremony this month, the pope proved himself more progressive than Nigel Farage when he encouraged women – not for the first time – to go ahead and breastfeed their children in the Sistine Chapel. Farage and others think women who might offend public sentiment by breastfeeding publicly should sit in a corner or perhaps cover themselves up with a massive napkin. Incidentally, women who think Farage offends public sentiment might suggest the same penalty for him. The pope's statement is a welcome step forward, though the need for such a proclamation is somewhat ironic when you consider that the Sistine Chapel itself is already copiously adorned with nudity, courtesy of Michelangelo.

Next, breasts once again threatened to eclipse women's achievements at the Golden Globe Awards, which spawned online headlines including 'Battle of the boobs!' and 'Whose boobs are hotter?' Perhaps inspired by the sheer intelligence of Seth MacFarlane's 2013 Oscars song 'We Saw Your Boobs', actor Jeremy Renner made a tired quip about Jennifer Lopez's 'globes' as he presented an award with her.

Meanwhile, contestant Jeremy Jackson was ejected from

the *Celebrity Big Brother* house after grabbing at model Chloe Goodman's dressing gown and exposing her breast. But despite the fact that police cautioned him for assault, other contestants were quick to criticize Goodman instead, with one, Ken Morley, accusing her of being 'naïve' and telling her: 'You're a single girl, you're twenty-one, you go into a room with a person you only know slightly, wearing only a robe. I think that's dodgy.' Another housemate, Alexander O'Neal, told her: 'I have to give it to you because I care. Living in an environment like this, with a group of men around you, there's no sneaky way to get dressed . . . You don't give no man a chance, I say it because I care but it was too much exposure.'

This all comes just days after the news that Rita Ora's choice of outfit (a jacket without a top underneath) for an interview on the BBC's *The One Show* sparked 400 complaints from affronted (pun intended) viewers. *The One Show* published an apology that sounded more like a ticking-off on its Facebook page, writing: 'We're sorry to those of you who were offended by Rita Ora's choice of outfit on yesterday's show. If we had been consulted on it we would have requested she wore something more suitable for 7pm.'

The *Daily Mail* website quickly produced an article about the resulting outrage, illustrated with eleven images and a video, as well as a further six photos of her in another low-cut dress, just for added context, of course. On the same day, the website reported another important story: 'Cheeky! Bikini-clad Rita Ora leaves VERY little to the imagination as she parties in next-to-nothing on luxury yacht.' To clear up any confusion, this was followed up with an article entitled: 'Little Miss look at me! How Rita Ora, the risqué new star of BBC's

The Voice – daughter of an Albanian pub landlord – has built a career out of outrageous attention-seeking.'

Not to be outdone, the *Daily Star* this week published an entire page of cleavage shots, minus their owners' faces, cunningly disguised as a quiz.

So, to recap, breasts imagined through a man's eyes and painted by his brush are high art, but women choosing to use these parts of their own bodies to feed their children are potentially offensive and must be policed by men. Women in show business are enormously pressured to reveal their bodies (which must conform to narrow media-dictated ideals) and to use sex appeal as a selling point. But those who choose to wear clothes they feel confident and happy in may be subject to anger and outrage, or be accused of being attention-seekers. The media is disgusted by such showing off, but will, nonetheless, heroically document each bikini moment with astonishing diligence. And though society repeatedly reminds us women's breasts are there primarily for men's pleasure and use, if women are assaulted they should realize it's their own fault for having breasts in the first place and wearing the wrong sort of clothes on them.

Glad we cleared that up.

Originally published 16 January 2015

'ARE YOU REALLY GOING TO EAT THAT?' YES, AND IT'S NOBODY ELSE'S BUSINESS

It all started with a single tweet:

> @emma_maier: was picking out chips at the store and a man told me 'Don't do it! You're so beautiful.' Let me buy my food in peace, dude.

After I retweeted the story, sent to the Everyday Sexism Twitter handle, I received reply after reply from other women, all detailing the same strange encounter. In each instance, a woman, about to consume some item of food, was suddenly and inexplicably confronted with unsolicited advice, usually from a male stranger, about the impact said morsel might have on her looks.

> @auntysarah: Getting breakfast at a hotel, a man I don't know sees me getting bacon and says, 'going for the diet option are we?'

> @SCSilk: Strangers telling me 'Don't eat that, you'll get fat'. Fries, ice cream.

> @jonanamary: sitting & eating outside a restaurant in Rouen, loitering man made continual comments eg 'look at her stuffing herself' :(

@jonanamary: He said nothing to my male
dinner companion, of course! But every
mouthful of bread – 'regarde comme elle
bouffe du pain' :(

@Safetyfox: bought chocolate from station
vending machine, bloke said 'moment on the
lips, lifetime on the hips'.

The instances vary, but only slightly. In most cases, the
exchange is strikingly uniform. The message, in almost every
case, is crystal clear: as a woman, your body is public property
and fair game for comment, instruction and policing.

This was so blatant, in fact, that in some cases the men even
cited specific societal 'requirements' and assumptions about
women's bodies in their comments:

@Mari_Fflur: Months before my wedding, I fill
my plate at a salad bar. Male colleague says
'Don't you have a wedding dress to fit into?'

@spunkyblah: I get told I 'don't need to drink
diet soda', as if being skinny is the only reason
to drink it.

Others quite openly made it clear that they felt a woman's food
consumption should be based entirely around how it might
impact on her attractiveness to men:

@chiara84: Have been told several times I
should eat more 'cause I'm too thin, and men
like to have 'something to squeeze'.

@THATissooAshley: was told to 'tone down'
concerning my taking plates full of food
at a buffet because 'boys won't like me'.
MANY TIMES.

This, really, is the key. That so many women have reported
this frankly quite incredibly patronizing experience is testa-
ment to the strength of the myth that a woman's physical form
exists, above all else, to titillate men. It's the same mistaken
assumption that lies behind the command to 'give us a smile',
or the belief that a woman in a low-cut top *must* be looking
for male attention.

As incredible as it seems, some women actually experience moments in their lives when their entire sentient being
isn't focused exclusively on providing men pleasure. They
might wear a strappy top because they are hot, for example;
eat a burger because they are hungry; or drink a diet soda
because they quite like the taste. Explosive revelations,
I know.

You might laugh, but for some, the belief that a man has an
automatic 'right' over the body of any woman he encounters
in a public space is worryingly ingrained. Take, for example,
this woman's account:

> @Molotovchicken: I was eating pasta salad on
> train. Guy walks over, grabs my food and
> throws it into bin. 'You shouldn't be eating that.'

This issue may not sound like a big one, but in fact it is closely interwoven with deeply damaging societal norms about women's bodies. The unrealistic and objectified images of women we are bombarded with daily already have a huge impact on women's body image and self-esteem. In a world in which many women experience near-constant anxiety about their bodies, having somebody you have never met before make a loaded comment about your weight just as you are on the point of eating something can be horribly unsettling. Several people tweeted that such encounters can trigger people who have had eating disorders. Others said it left them feeling too judged and uncomfortable to eat in public.

Even when the comment doesn't directly reference weight, there is a heavily implied sort of disgust or shock at the idea of a woman eating:

> @chazma85: all the time, eating chips recently
> and a man said 'Bloody hell, you can't get
> them down you quick enough can you?'

And, of course, as with so many other impossible standards, women simply can't win:

> @flumpmistress: Yes! Vending machines – so
> often a random male stranger around to ask:
> 'Should you be eating that?' #EverydaySexism

@nicnaclala: And sometimes the opposite if
I'm eating a salad – you need more than that,
have a cake!

The normalization of this bizarre belief that a woman's choice of lunch is a public matter is exacerbated by its reflection in the media. 'Not a model meal' crowed one *Daily Mail* headline, after Helena Christensen had been caught in the shocking act of eating a sandwich. 'Pregnant Kim Kardashian succumbs to cravings and gorges on burger and chips' shrieked another headline, after the then-pregnant reality star stopped the press by having lunch. And of course, the words drip with the implicit greed of the women – Christensen 'feasts', Kardashian 'gorges'. The close connections with body-shaming are there too – the *Mail* solemnly warns that Christensen 'had better be careful with her eating habits in the future' in case she ruins her model figure (reminder: she ate a sandwich). And in case we weren't all completely clear that attracting men is a woman's sole function, and that it's only our bodies men are interested in, it even continues: 'She could end up losing the famous 35–24–35 measurements that have made her the toast of men everywhere, including her current partner, Interpol frontman Paul Banks.' Summary: woman eats sandwich, may get dumped by husband for getting fat.

One can only hope that the world will eventually come to terms with the shocking revelation that women do, in fact, eat meals, so that such vital headlines may one day become a thing of the past. In the meantime, I'd suggest following the excellent example of these tweeters:

@PyroClaire: A colleague criticized my food
for a couple of months. I asked him if [it]
was because I'm office junior or a woman.
He stopped.

@LinziSue: Bloke: I find women who drink pints
unattractive. Me: Great, I didn't want to attract
you. *buys another pint*

Originally published 24 July 2014

WHY SHOULD WOMEN RUN THE GAUNTLET OF HARASSMENT WHILE OUT JOGGING?

When out jogging, leering and lewd comments from men you've never met, as they whizz by in their cars, is exactly the kind of 'encouragement' that women dread. Yet, despite the fairly obvious fact that none of us appreciates harassment at the best of times, let alone when we're gasping up a steep incline or making our way around a deserted park, it is at precisely these moments that many women find themselves the target of it.

For those who haven't experienced sexual harassment this might sound shocking, but to many women it is the price they pay for simply choosing to jog, cycle or exercise outside. Plenty of women have posted on Everyday Sexism with similar experiences:

'As I was running to my local swimming pool, a car slowed down beside me and a guy shouted "whore" at me.'

'Was outside trying to enjoy a run, and in the hour I spent in public, got honked and/or shouted at no less than three times.'

'I do exercise classes outside in a public park. Teenagers on bicycles yelling obscenities. Middle-aged men leering openly as I stretch. Men old enough to be my father saying things that make it clear that I'm obviously only there for them to look at.'

'Cycling up Stamford Hill last Friday, a man grins at me, saying "lucky saddle". I'm forty-one, and heard exactly the same phrase when I was cycling to school at sixteen.'

From comments about weight loss and women's figures

to sexually explicit invitations and aggressive verbal abuse, women find themselves facing a veritable barrage of unwanted attention. And the problem doesn't stop there; in many instances it escalates further:

'Just had my crotch grabbed at by man on bike whilst I was jogging in north London.'

'I was cycling alone on a secluded road near my house a few years ago, I was about fourteen. A car drove up beside me, at speed and less than a foot away and a man reached out and grabbed my bum, nearly pushing me off the bike.'

'I was out running by a canal recently. I ran past a man walking in the other direction who used the narrow path to his advantage and managed to grab a feel of my bum as I ran past.'

The problem is so bad that many women describe the coping mechanisms they adopt, from avoiding certain routes, to playing loud music through headphones to avoid hearing harassment. Many even said they had given up on exercise altogether in order to avoid it.

'I live in north London. I used to run on a regular basis but no longer enjoy going because of the number of comments I receive.'

'I want to take up jogging but without a buddy too intimi-dated due to previous experience of heckling.'

'Just had to cut my run short & go home as felt very unsafe due to men driving past and slowing down, beeping and shouting obscenities at me out the window. I was out for five minutes. How is this fair?'

According to Sport England, 2 million more men than women play regular sport. Meanwhile only 31 per cent of

14-year-old girls do regular exercise, compared to 50 per cent of boys the same age.

The good news is that a number of women have described positive experiences after choosing to report incidents. The runner whose bottom was grabbed as she ran along the canal, wrote: 'A few days later I called the police as I couldn't get it out of my head that he had been there to prey on women, using the narrow path to his advantage. I thought the police would laugh at me for reporting something so minor, but they took it very seriously. They were even a bit cross I hadn't called it in at the time. They came and took a full statement and will now have more officers out on the canal path to watch out for the joggers.'

Another said: 'While out running on a reasonably busy street in broad daylight, I was stopped and asked for directions . . . I obliged and as I showed him on the map on my phone he looked down my top, made a sleazy remark then grabbed my breast . . . I calmly took his registration and went straight to the police. I was surprised by how seriously they took it. They thanked me for coming in! They agreed with me: this guy was out of order and his behaviour was not okay! He's been charged.'

However, not everybody feels able to report incidents to the police, and it would be helpful to see more bystanders stepping in to challenge harassment, as they are often in a stronger position to do so than the victim. It is ludicrous that women are still made to feel scared, hounded and unsafe exercising in public spaces. And for anyone who thinks that harassing a jogger is a great romantic approach, this runner has the perfect response:

@deepoceandive: Big thanks to the guy who decided to follow, imitate & mock me whilst I was running :):) I now want to have your babies!!! #everydaysexism

Originally published 20 August 2015

THE MORNING-AFTER PILL IS SAFE. SO WHY IS IT SO DIFFICULT TO ACCESS?

A new campaign from the British Pregnancy Advisory Service (BPAS) is calling for emergency contraception, commonly known as the morning-after pill, to be sold directly from pharmacy shelves without a mandatory consultation. The campaign highlights the fact that the pill can cost British women up to £30, as much as five times higher than in other European countries, meaning that it could even be cheaper to fly to France and buy it there than to visit a local pharmacy.

A 2003 report published in the *Pharmaceutical Journal* revealed that the high price – described by BPAS chief executive Ann Furedi as a 'sexist surcharge' – was a deliberate attempt to prevent women from taking it too often. As a spokesperson for Levonelle, a manufacturer of the pill, said: 'The price has been set, in part, to ensure that EHC [emergency hormonal contraception] is not used as a regular method of contraception.'

BPAS also argues that the mandatory consultation women must go through with a pharmacist may be part of the reason it is so costly in the UK, compared with other countries where such consultations are not required. Given that the medication is considered very safe, even compared with other medications sold off the shelf, and that the NHS says it has no serious side effects, it seems likely that this is a means of influencing women's sexual and reproductive decisions, rather than a requirement for safety reasons.

The comments of one spokesman from the Family

Education Trust exemplified this rationale: 'With no questions asked about previous medical history or previous use of the drug, there is a very real danger that it could be misused or overused.' The same could be said of countless other off-the-shelf products, but the extra barriers only seem to come into play when a product is associated with female sexuality. And considering the lack of medical dangers associated with the morning-after pill, the 'misuse' or 'overuse' seems likely to be a moral, rather than medical, judgement.

So the major arguments both for the sky-high cost and the mandatory consultation seem closely tied to the idea that women cannot be trusted to make their own decisions about their bodies and sex lives. Not to mention the terrifying risk that, should the situation change, immoral, promiscuous women might run amok, foregoing other forms of contraception, indulging in countless one-night stands and choosing to pop morning-after pills instead of taking any other precautions.

Of course, it makes sense for a consultation to be available for those who choose it, as with any other product purchased in a pharmacy. Some people might want to ask about the efficacy of the medication within a given timeframe, or seek further information about issues such as sexually transmitted diseases. But this is a decision an individual is capable of making herself – not every person taking emergency contraception needs to be subjected to these interactions, often described as 'embarrassing' and 'shaming'.

The moralistic overtones of this debate are the same ones that emerge during any discussion relating to women's reproductive health – as if male lawmakers and commentators feel the need to wrestle women's autonomy from them because 'we know best'.

As a healthcare option for those who wish to avoid unwanted pregnancy, it is important that women should be able to access the morning-after pill as easily and cheaply as possible. But a 2014 study published in the *European Journal of Contraception and Reproductive Health Care* found that women in the UK were nearly twice as unlikely to use emergency contraception because they were 'embarrassed to ask for it' than women in other European countries. Nearly a third of all the women surveyed who used emergency contraception said they felt uncomfortable or judged when obtaining it.

That women have to jump through hoops because they aren't trusted to use it responsibly is reminiscent of the ongoing Victorian-era legislation that means abortion is still technically illegal in mainland Britain. Rather than overturning the 1861 Offences Against the Person Act, the 1967 Abortion Act essentially created a loophole allowing the procedure only after two doctors have agreed that a woman's mental or physical health would be harmed by continuing with the pregnancy. The law hasn't been changed since.

Like the idea that a woman's decision isn't valid until two doctors have agreed to 'let her off' prosecution, the notion that we need a consultation before being allowed to take emergency contraception is outdated and patronizing. Isn't it time we moved away from the Victorian notion that women can't be trusted to make their own choices about their health, bodies and sex lives?

Originally published 30 November 2016

IT'S NOT GROPING OR FONDLING – IT IS SEXUAL ASSAULT

Numerous high-profile cases of sexual violence and abuse have been exposed in recent years, with the same words cropping up again and again: 'groping', 'fondling', 'inappropriate touching'. What each of these terms usually means is sexual assault. But both in casual conversation and in the press, we will go to almost any lengths to avoid saying it.

According to the Sexual Offences Act 2003, the elements of the offence of sexual assault are:

- A person (A) intentionally touches another person (B)
- The touching is sexual
- (B) does not consent to the touching, and (A) does not reasonably believe that (B) consents.

The Crown Prosecution Service guidelines further clarify that 'touching is widely defined and includes with any part of the body, or with anything else, and can be through clothing'.

Sometimes, the reason behind a reluctance to use accurate language is more compassionate than malicious – an attempt to avoid the reality of what happens to girls and women on a regular basis. It is easier to rely on euphemistic language, such as 'groping' or 'fondling', than to talk about sexual assault. But that doesn't help, because we inadvertently end up downgrading the severity of the offence, which, in turn, helps to normalize it.

Undermining sexual violence through diminishing

language is prevalent but not new. Consider, for example, the popular online meme that states: 'It's not rape, it's a struggle snuggle.' It's a trivialization that leads to a culture where victims are doubted and/or blamed. Was it really sexual assault, or just a quick caress? Are you honestly going to make a fuss about a pat on the bottom? Sure, he's the president-elect, but lighten up, he was only joking about grabbing women by the pussy! It's the sort of language that allows a mainstream television programme to 'debate' the acceptability of sexual assault using a question such as: 'Is a bum pinch harmless fun?'

By not pointing out how unacceptable this culture is, we become complicit in the message that victims are already receiving loud and clear: this isn't really a big deal, you won't be taken seriously, it's not worth going to the police. According to aggregated data from the Crime Survey for England and Wales between 2009 and 2012, one of the most frequently cited reasons for not reporting sexual offences is that they seemed 'too trivial' to report.

It is a message so entrenched in society that the vast majority of women and girls are completely unaware that being touched on the breasts, grabbed between the legs or squeezed on the bottom, among other common experiences, could constitute sexual assault. Many girls come to see this behaviour as normal – expected even – and simply the price you pay for being a woman. This not only means that victims are much less likely to report what has happened (or feel able to complain in a workplace, nightclub or school setting), but also that perpetrators are unaware of the severity of committing such offences.

Unfortunately, the term 'sexual assault' has become so

little understood that it is sometimes necessary to talk about 'touching' or 'grabbing' in order to elicit accurate responses. Far fewer people might report 'sexual assault' in a survey, for example, than would describe having been touched without their consent.

Words such as 'groping' and 'fondling' are incapable of carrying the weight of the experiences they are stretched to encompass: an elderly woman pinned roughly against a wall in her home by a friend of her late husband; an 11-year-old girl too afraid to report the male classmate stroking the inside of her thigh under the desk during a geography lesson; a university student out running when a passer-by grabbed her suddenly and firmly by the breasts; a video store cashier whose boss would smack her bottom each time she went up the ladder to the storeroom. All stories that have been relayed to me personally, some through tears. A litany of sexual assaults, reduced to something flimsy and dismissible. Moments that profoundly affect women's lives, diminished and whitewashed.

Language has such power. When we deny victims the words to describe and define their own experiences, we actively disempower them and distance them from justice. We owe it to all survivors to start describing 'groping' and 'fondling' by their real name: sexual assault.

Originally published 13 January 2017

WHY WOMEN NEED TO SHOUT ABOUT SEXUAL PLEASURE

Over 50 per cent of women would like to be having more sex, according to a recent survey of users of the fertility app Kindara. Contrary to popular stereotypes about men having higher sex drives than women, 75 per cent of the 500 women polled would like to be having sex more than three times a week, and 13 per cent would prefer six times per week.

The survey comes hot on the heels of a new Tumblr called How to Make Me Come, which has been making waves by sharing women's intimate accounts of sex and orgasm, in their own words.

'Kissing me will make me feel like I am more than a vagina (which I am),' begins one essay.

Another says: 'Giving the direction "fingers inside me with clitoral stimulation" seemed to cause as much confusion as telling him to look behind something to find the milk.'

It might seem like the idea of women enjoying, demanding and taking the lead in sex is hardly a revolutionary concept these days, but it could be argued that the advent of online pornography has turned back the clock on the sexual revolution, at least from a feminist perspective. I speak to girls at school who have seen porn on boys' mobile phones and think that sex is something at best aggressive, at worst violent; something that will be done to them when they 'give in'; something that men initiate and perform for their own pleasure while women submit. I have spoken to boys who have seen it and are confused and bewildered by the role they feel will be expected of them. One young woman who wrote to me had been having sex with her boyfriend for the first time when, with no warning, he started trying to throttle her. Shocked and scared, she managed to push him away. But it was he who broke down in relief, asking her: 'Wasn't that what you were expecting?'

Sexual empowerment and feminism remain closely linked in a world in which women are expected to perform sexually but not necessarily to make their own demands. The idea of the personal space as political remains deeply relevant while we still battle to extend the popular understanding of rape beyond the mythical shadowy stranger in a dark alleyway.

As we debate consent at university and contend with the deliberately obtuse who suggest it is unfair to expect a man to explain how he knew a woman consented, the notion of consensual, empowered female pleasure is one we need to shout about.

The reclamation of sexual control is complex, particularly in light of the centuries-old exotification and colonization of the bodies of women of colour, the erasure of sexual orientations and gender identities that fall outside the heteronormative, gender essentialist mainstream, and the prejudice and violence faced by sex workers and trans women.

What feels like sexual empowerment to one woman doesn't necessarily look the same to another. For example, the idea of a woman instructing a partner in the specifics of how to turn her on might feel different for women who are already battling sexual stereotypes associated with their race, profession, sexuality or gender identity. But it is exciting and important that spaces are opening up for women to speak out in their own words, publicly (and sometimes anonymously), about what was once considered stigmatized and taboo.

How to Make Me Come isn't the only platform offering women a space to speak openly about their sexual experiences – the sharing of personal stories is also an integral part of Pavan Amara's My Body Back Project, which supports survivors of sexual violence to reclaim their bodies. For some women, taking back the narrative of sex is a crucial part of regaining control. Alongside its Café V workshops and health clinics, My Body Back also offers free poetry and creative-writing workshops, which aim to help women reclaim their physicality through their own words. Amara says: 'After any sort of sexual violence, the way you think about sex and your body changes, so you think it's not under your control or you have to go with somebody else's likes and dislikes and you lose that connection to yourself. We looked at taking that back.'

We live in a world in which the ubiquity of the male gaze constantly packages women for sexualized consumption, yet the notion of women enjoying their own sexuality remains startling to some.

The fact that so many women disclosed their sexual desires to an app doesn't necessarily mean that they feel similarly confident relaying them to their sexual partners – in fact, their reported dissatisfaction might suggest otherwise.

In the age of online porn, which shows women going from zero to panting with next to no foreplay and having suspiciously regular screaming simultaneous orgasms with very little apparent effort from their partners, for women to share their stories about sex and climax isn't just powerful. It's a public service.

Originally published 24 September 2015

SCHOOL DRESS CODES REINFORCE THE MESSAGE THAT WOMEN'S BODIES ARE DANGEROUS

As pupils go back to school this month, one institution has hit the headlines for sending up to 150 girls home for wearing skirts that were deemed 'too short'. Pupils at Tring School in Hertfordshire were either placed in seclusion or had to be picked up by their parents, reported ITV news.

A statement from Tring School's headteacher, Sue Collings, said: 'We believe that students looking smart and professional is an important element of being a successful school. We also believe that, if students are consistently dressed in the correct uniform, it enables us to focus on teaching and learning. As such, we have a school uniform policy that has been in place for some time that is adhered to by the large majority of the students. The most contentious issue, though, is the style and length of the skirt worn by the girls.' It also stressed that parents and pupils had been warned in advance that uniform regulations would be tightened after a decision by school leadership in the summer.

But parents commenting below the statement on the school's Facebook page expressed frustration at their struggle to find skirts that would fit their daughters' waists while fulfilling the length requirement. Some said their daughters' heights or body shapes simply made the skirt sit higher. One parent commented: 'My daughter wore "regular", not skinny, trousers from a school uniform shop, they had no external pockets as per guidance and [she] was told they showed every bone in her body and was put in internal for four lessons today.' On another post, a parent said her daughter had been forced to wear a skirt several sizes too big safety-pinned round her waist in order to obey the length requirement.

Tring wasn't the only school to take such measures – other reports have described children being sent home from various schools in the past week for wearing the wrong footwear, or even the wrong kind of socks. But while boys have been punished for some dress code violations too, it is clear that the majority of cases involve girls' appearance being policed.

A number of pupils at South Shields Community College were made to change because their trousers were deemed 'too tight'. And these cases follow hot on the heels of two schools that have banned female pupils from wearing skirts altogether. In May, Bridlington School in East Yorkshire reportedly banned skirts after a male staff member was made to feel 'uncomfortable' when implementing rules over their length. And in July it was reported that Trentham High School in Stoke-on-Trent was banning skirts, with the head teacher saying: 'It's not pleasant for male members of staff and students either, the girls have to walk up stairs and sit down and it's a complete distraction.' This week, the same school is reported to have sent home ten girls whose trousers were deemed too tight because they would prove a 'distraction' to male teachers.

The media images of the Tring schoolgirls in their 'inappropriate' skirts, worn over thick black tights, powerfully remind me of another recent case, in which a US teenager was sent home from school for wearing an outfit that revealed her collarbones. What is so shocking, or offensive, about the bottom inch of a teenage girl's thigh, or the bones below her neck?

In fact, that case was just the latest in a recent string of high-profile dress code battles in the US and Canada, where students have been protesting for some time about dress codes that unfairly target girls, using the hashtag #IAmMoreThanADistraction and turning up at school with placards asking: 'Are my pants lowering your test scores?'

While the principle of asking students to attend school smartly dressed sounds reasonable, the problem comes when wider sexist attitudes towards women and their bodies are projected on to young women by schools in their attempt to define what constitutes smartness. It's no coincidence that many school dress codes contain far more rules pertaining to girls' clothing than to boys', as we live in a world where women's bodies are policed and fought over to a far greater extent than men's. When girls are denied time in the classroom because their knees, shoulders or upper arms are considered inappropriate and in need of covering up, it privileges the societal sexualization of their adolescent bodies over their own right to learn. We don't have the same qualms about seeing those parts of their male peers' anatomy.

Meanwhile, the repeated use of the word 'distracting' centres the needs of men and boys above those of the girls, and suggests that girls' bodies are powerful and dangerous, impacting on boys and teachers, whose behaviour is implicitly excused as inevitable. It is girls' responsibility to cover up, not men and boys' responsibility to restrain themselves. If male teachers are 'distracted' by pupils' legs then I would suggest that the girls' trousers are not the main thing we need to be worried about.

Then there is the potentially negative impact of draconian

dress codes on trans or gender non-conforming pupils, many of whom have reported being blocked from their school year-books because of clothing choices.

Another common refrain is that it is important to prepare pupils for the 'world of work' – this was the explanation given by the headmaster of Ryde Academy on the Isle of Wight last year when more than 250 girls were taken out of lessons because their skirts were too short. But if schools pull girls out of lessons and publicly shame them for exposing too much of their bodies, they are only preparing them for a sexist and unfair working world in which women are constantly judged and berated on their appearance. Men, by comparison, get a free pass. Look at the endless articles about whether women 'should' or 'shouldn't' wear make-up to be taken seriously at work, or cringeworthy instructions from firms on how female staff should dress.

Wouldn't it be refreshing to see a school taking a stand against the idea that girls' bodies are irresistibly dangerous and sexualized, instead of reinforcing it?

Originally published 10 September 2015

#NotAllMen

Poor, beleaguered men. They're not all bad, you know. Well of course you know. Not a single feminist I have ever met actually needs this pointed out to them. In fact, the only people who actually seem to buy into the idea that there's some ideological war on all men are the ones writing articles with titles like 'American men are being institutionally oppressed' and '"White Men": the most dehumanizing insult of our times'. Feminists, who spend their lives fighting against the notion that an entire group of people are the same simply because of their sex, are unsurprisingly not trying to smear all men as sexist pigs. They are, however, interested in tackling many issues, from sexual violence to street harassment to stalking, which undeniably involve a disproportionate number of male perpetrators and female victims.

To acknowledge this is not to implicate all men in criminal or sexist behaviour, nor to deny the devastating experiences of male survivors of sexual violence. It is to recognize a system of oppression that is rooted in gender inequality and whose structural nature must be named in order for it to be tackled effectively.

It is not counter-intuitive to fight for a feminism grounded in an awareness of the systemic and institutional nature of female oppression, and at the same time to recognize the ways in which gender inequality impacts negatively on some individual men. It is possible to acknowledge the fantastic contributions made by some men in the battle against sexism and at the same time to realize that the majority of perpetrators of sexism and sexual abuse are men, raised in a system that grooms them for patriarchal privilege just as it prepares girls for objectification and subjugation.

EDUCATION IS ESSENTIAL FOR CHANGING MALE ATTITUDES TOWARDS SEXUAL VIOLENCE

'My name is Nicola, I am thirteen and I am so scared to have sex it makes me cry nearly every day.'

So starts an entry to the Everyday Sexism Project from a schoolgirl who has seen videos of 'sex' (she doesn't use the word porn) on her peers' mobile phones at school. She continues: 'It looks so horrible and like it hurts ... I feel like it's unfair that girls have to have horrible things done to them but boys can just laugh and watch the videos and they don't realize how scary it is ... the real-life sex that we see is so scary and painful and the woman is crying and getting hurt' [sic].

Another girl's entry reads: 'Yesterday at school I was sat at a desk working, and didn't notice a male friend of mine take a picture of my breasts. The only reason I found out is because he snap-chatted the picture to various other guys from my school, having edited it so that my breasts were circled.'

One entry comes from a girl who describes being sexually assaulted at school at the age of twelve. She writes: 'I can't type too much because I'm starting to cry, but suffice to say he put his hands in places that I did not want him to.'

Another is written by a teacher and form tutor in a secondary school. It says: 'I witness on a daily basis the girls in my classes being called "whore", "bitch", "slag", "slut" as a matter of course, heckled if they dare to speak in class, their shirts being forcibly undone and their skirts being lifted and held by groups of boys (I WANT TO EMPHASIZE THAT

THIS IS MORE OFTEN THAN NOT A DAILY EVENT, AND OFTEN BORDERS ON ASSAULT). On a daily basis, I am forced to confiscate mobile phones as boys are watching hardcore pornography videos in lessons and I have noticed, sadly, that as time has gone on the girls in my classes have become more and more reserved and reluctant to draw attention to themselves.'

From online porn to page 3, Facebook memes to *Game of Thrones*, young people in the UK are growing up facing a barrage of ideas and information about sex and gender, what it means to be a man or a woman, and how they will be judged and valued as adults. Data from a 2010 YouGov survey for the End Violence Against Women coalition found that 71 per cent of 16–18-year-olds have heard sexual name-calling to girls at school at least a few times a week. Among the same age group, almost one in three girls had experienced unwanted sexual touching at school. According to a 2009 NSPCC report, one in three girls aged 13–17 reported sexual partner violence, a quarter reported physical partner violence and nearly three-quarters reported emotional partner violence.

We know young people are facing all this and more, yet we don't give them the basic tools to help them analyse and make sense of the material with which they are confronted. The government recently rejected proposals to make age-appropriate sex education on issues such as sexual relationships, violence and consent compulsory on the school curriculum. For boys and girls, an alternate narrative is desperately needed in the classroom, so that received ideas from misogynistic videos and websites aren't accepted as the facts of what 'real-life sex' and relationships must look like. We know that a woman in the UK has a one in four chance of experiencing domestic violence, yet we don't teach our children about healthy relationships. We know that 85,000 women are raped every year but consent isn't on the curriculum.

This week, I'll travel to Kosovo to observe the work of the Young Men initiative, a project supported by the charity Care International. The idea behind the initiative is simple: by educating young men on issues such as gender equality, violence and sex, they become part of the solution rather than part of the problem. In the wake of its success so far, governments in Croatia, Serbia and Kosovo have added compulsory teaching of these issues to the curriculum. Now, Care International is calling on governments around the world to follow suit. Ahead of June's global summit to end sexual violence in conflict, the charity has launched a petition asking the summit's co-chairs, William Hague and Angelina Jolie, to urge ministers from the 140 countries attending the summit to ensure these vital issues are covered in the classroom.

Alice Allan, head of advocacy at Care International UK, said: 'We'll never end sexual violence – whether it's happening in war zones or behind closed doors here in the UK – without tackling the root causes. The attitudes that lead to abuse and sickening attacks on women and girls are ingrained in society, globally. Care's work has shown that working with men and boys really can break the cycle of violence. In parts of the Balkans, where teaching boys and young men about respect, consent and non-violence in relationships is already on the curriculum, 73 per cent now say it is wrong to use violence against an unfaithful partner, compared with 48 per cent before. This is just the start but it's clear that educating young men and boys to change male attitudes is a crucial step to ending violence against women in the next generation.'

It's a call to arms to which the UK should be first to respond. This isn't to suggest that every boy is part of the problem. Indeed, many men will experience violence and assault themselves. Rather, it's about the radical idea that men and boys have the opportunity to be part of the change, within a society that needs to see a dramatic cultural shift in the very idea of what it means to be a man.

Again and again, when incidents of sexual violence are reported, society blames the victim. We hear countless calls to warn girls: don't wear a short skirt, don't go out late at night, don't walk alone, and yet the rapes and assaults continue. Because contrary to popular belief, it isn't the victims that cause them at all. It's time we started educating boys.

Originally published 30 May 2014

THE MEN WHO HELP FIGHT BACK AGAINST EVERYDAY SEXISM

On the eve of International Women's Day, Phumzile Mlambo-Ngcuka, the UN under-secretary general, penned a powerful and rousing open letter urging men and boys to stand alongside women in the fight for gender equality. Highlighting the new UN Women HeForShe campaign, she outlined the practical reasons why working to eradicate sexism is in everybody's interest – from strengthening economies to reducing world hunger. She also appealed to men to recognize that gender inequality impacts on those nearest and dearest to them – their mothers, sisters, friends and daughters. But, most importantly, she pointed out that standing up for gender equality is quite simply the right thing to do.

The following morning, my first tweet about celebrating International Women's Day was met immediately with a predictable reply from a male tweeter: 'When's national men's day?' But before I could respond, one of my male followers jumped in: 'I know, right??? When's MY day? Why isn't every day about me? A whole day! Once a year! Where will it end?' In a second tweet, he continued: 'Also it's November the 19th. That took a second on Google. BUT THESE BLOODY WOMEN, EH?' Without for one moment disparaging the importance of International Men's Day, which focuses on issues such as men's and boys' health, gender equality and positive male role models, I appreciated the support from a male ally who was prepared to stand alongside us in defending the importance of International Women's Day.

Since starting the Everyday Sexism Project two years ago, I've heard from many men about their own unique, personal ways of standing up to sexism. One had written to the chairman of his football club to protest the violent misogyny in the regular chants he heard at matches. Another, after reading the website and realizing the serious impact street harassment has on many victims, chased after the next man he saw shouting at women in the street, tapped him on the shoulder, and asked him: 'Why did you do that?'

One man wrote: 'I am a 22-year-old male. I cannot stop reading this website ... More and more I find myself calling out men when they make these comments. It isn't easy, and one instance will not change their behaviour. However, I think it does make a difference ... Will encourage other men to stop this behaviour when they see it.' Another said: 'I have been ridiculed many times for speaking up about it, but now I know I am not alone I will be speaking up a lot more.' In that spirit of solidarity, this week on Twitter we asked our followers to share their stories of men standing up against sexism, to celebrate them, and more importantly to encourage others to do the same.

Some people suggested that it was wrong to celebrate instances of men standing up to sexism, when this should be the bare minimum of what we expect. But while I agree that simply not being sexist should absolutely be the norm, the act of taking a public stand against discrimination, of loudly calling it out, of challenging your peers, or stepping in when witnessing public harassment, is not always easy and deserves to be celebrated. Yes, some of these actions are minor, but the whole point of Everyday Sexism is that much of what we are fighting is apparently 'minor' – it is insidious and ingrained, and the smallest acts can start the vital shift we need to combat it. Just as the mosaic of Everyday Sexism is made up of tiny pinpricks, so too the solution can consist of joining the tiniest of dots. And though, as feminist activists, we think about these things all the time and it is easy to become frustrated when others are slower to react, for many people even the very act of becoming aware of gender inequality can be a major paradigm shift, let alone beginning to take steps towards combating it.

If we are to be pragmatic about creating the real change we want to see, we should encourage these actions. Take the high school teacher who spent a class explaining some of the vital facts underlying gender inequality to his students. Yes, this might seem a relatively simple act but if every teacher did the same thing, it would be an enormous step in the right direction. The same principle of scale could be applied to many of the tweets we received.

'Guy at a hotel gave me "that look" and said: "Helloooo" to me. His friend said: "Don't be a dick" – need more guys like that.'

'My husband always challenges sexism. He doesn't want our daughter experiencing some of the things I have.'

'I keep asking "Why is that funny?" and "I don't get it" when guys make sexist jokes. Embarrasses them as they explain it.'

'My 12yo son learned to do laundry and cook because he wants his someday-wife to have respect for me.'

'The boy in the park today, who, when his friend started making sexist comments, told him to shut up and stop being a dick.'

'My high school teacher took a class to explain the difference of sex and gender, the problems of binarism & stereotyping.'

'My brother, who identifies himself as a feminist and who challenges casual sexism and misogyny relentlessly.'

'My 18-yr-old son who walked out of work placement disgusted by degrading images of women. It meant the world to me.'

'Group of drunk lads shouted "Get yer tits out" to woman a few yards ahead of me so I lifted my T-shirt and showed them mine.'

And if sharing these stories spurs other men on to follow the same example, then so much the better.

Originally published 14 March 2014

DO YOU DO THE IRONING OR DO YOU TAKE OUT THE BINS? IT MAY BE TIME TO GENDER-SWAP YOUR CHORES

A fortnight ago, I received the following tweet: 'Husband casually mentioned today he has never cleaned our bathroom – it's always me! How did I miss that for 31 years?!' Apart from chortling at one response ('You were too busy cleaning the bathroom!'), the thing that struck me about the tweet was just how much it resonated with my own experiences and those I had heard from other women.

Even among feminist friends and forward-thinking families, it's fascinating to see how our insistence on gender equality in every other area of life sometimes falters before the stubborn persistence of gendered chores. This goes both for the type of tasks (who does the laundry and washes up? Who takes out the bins?) and the quantity of time spent doing them. A recent BBC survey found that women spend twice as much time on chores as men, devoting well over the equivalent of one working day per week to household duties. And a Mumsnet survey of 1,000 working mothers found that only 5 per cent of men took responsibility for giving the house a weekly clean, compared with 71 per cent of women. The stark division in unpaid labour also encompasses childcare – from who looks after children at weekends to who is expected to take time off when children are sick – and persists even in surveys of heterosexual couples where the male partner doesn't have a job. Among same-sex couples, some studies have suggested that there is likely to be a fairer division of chores, while others seem to suggest there is still a somewhat 'gendered' division of labour, with the lower-earning partner tending to take on chores traditionally considered 'women's work', such as cooking.

The extra burden usually taken on by women in hetero-sexual couples also includes 'emotional labour', such as keeping on top of a child's progress at school, checking in with elderly relatives and organizing social events, adding to the so-called 'second shift' millions of women work, often without thanks or acknowledgement. Many would argue that the reason the divide has persisted so long is because it is unimportant – as long as you maintain a healthy, respectful relationship, you might ask, who cares who does the DIY or cleans the loo?

But the division of chores plays into myriad other prob-lems, from the assumption that women are better suited to caring professions to the struggle for shared parental leave. Recently, it was even suggested that women's shouldering of extra domestic work alongside full-time employment might be contributing to the slowing growth pace of female life expectancy!

Of course, in many families men do help, or do their fair share of the chores, but such stereotypes can still be insidi-ous in forming young people's ideas about the world and the importance of men's and women's time. You can see these ideas reflected later on, in issues such as the expectation that women will always make the tea in the workplace, the idea that a woman is 'lucky' if her partner helps out with 'babysitting' his own children, or the societal pressure for women to sacrifice career for child-rearing. The impact is startlingly wide.

It might be an eye-opening experiment to take note of the chores being done over the next two weeks and then attempt to 'gender-swap' some or all of them (children's tasks included) over the next year. Even the most forward-thinking among us might be surprised, after stopping to add it up, about just what is going on inside our own homes.

Originally published 8 January 2016

FIVE WAYS TO MAKE
MARRIAGE MORE EQUAL

David Cameron has asked the Home Office to change the content of marriage registers in England and Wales to include details of mothers as well as fathers. It has taken more than a year of feminist campaigning to bring this issue to prominence, since Ailsa Burkimsher Sadler instigated a Change.org petition calling for mothers' names to be added, in August 2013. Ending the invisibility of women's identities in these historical documents is an important step forward, practically and symbolically, but there are many other elements of modern marriage that could be updated to achieve equality.

1. Proposals

You might hope we were past the stage at which women were expected to sit around, twiddling their thumbs and waiting for the man in their life to take full responsibility for steering their shared future, yet I've still heard tutted responses about 'what a shame' it is and even 'how embarrassing' when female friends have been the ones to propose. It is mind-boggling that there is still such a stigma around the idea of a woman in a heterosexual couple being the one to pop the question. Gone are the days of knights in shining armour and rescued princesses, so is it not time women were allowed to play an equal role in determining their own futures?

2. The looks obsession

The dress of your dreams. The heavenly hairstyle. Shoes! Shoes! Shoes! You can read a bridal magazine from cover to glossy cover without ever touching on a single idea outside of the all-encompassing importance of a woman's looks on her wedding day. Sure, most will want to look nice, but our societal obsession with the beauty of the bride, from the toasts to the photographs, makes it easy for a woman's personality and the commitment she is making to get completely lost in superficial objectification. One instant way to remedy this? Turn another ancient, misogynistic tradition on its head and have the bride give a speech at her own wedding (and preferably plenty of other women too). At least that way she gets a voice, instead of being a demure, mute object of admiration.

3. Domestic chores

If we really want to talk seriously about marriage equality, it is not weddings we should be looking at, but marriages themselves. Analysis published by the Institute for Public Policy Research in 2012 indicated that 77 per cent of married women do more housework than their husbands, while just one in ten married men do an equal amount of housework as their wives. Yet the idea of cooking, washing and cleaning as 'women's work' is an archaic norm that is so insidious it is difficult to challenge. On a recent school visit a class of 7- and 8-year-olds, the children were quick to tell me that sport, politics and maths were all 'boy things'. I asked them what they felt 'girl things' were, thinking they might point to literature, or drama perhaps? My heart sank as they answered:

'Cooking, cleaning, tidying.' Why such strong stereotypes at such a young age? Well, just look at the heavy gendering of children's cookery and cleaning toys, for a start.

4. Childcare

Women also take on the majority of caring duties for children and other relatives. According to employment figures from April to June 2013, having a baby makes men significantly more likely to be employed but women far less likely, suggesting that this inequality may be having a major impact on women's employment. New shared parental leave rules that come into force next year should help to alleviate the pressure on women to take on the lion's share of caring for a new baby. However, prohibitively expensive childcare, a lack of flexible working hours and cultural prejudice still mean it's far more likely to be women who pay the career-limiting price for having a family. And, of course, this inequality applies outside marriage, too.

5. Decision-making

One of the most commonly reported scenarios to the Everyday Sexism Project is a woman taking a phone call from a lettings agent, double-glazing salesman or bank employee who asks 'Is your husband in?' Or being told: 'I can't discuss this without your husband present.' The days of women in the UK needing a husband's support to take out a loan or buy a car may be over, but the prejudiced assumption that men should control household decisions has not faded just yet, and it has a very real impact on women's ability to run their own lives.

Originally published 19 August 2014

WHAT WOMEN ARE STILL
PUTTING UP WITH AT WORK

If there's anywhere people want to convince themselves that we've already solved sexism, it's in the workplace. I can't count the number of well-meaning men who've earnestly explained to me that there just *isn't* any sexism in their line of work (law, media, medicine) any more. And for every one of those men who slightly patronizingly explains to me that the problem doesn't exist, because they'd know about it if it was happening under their noses, I hear from several hundred female lawyers, journalists or doctors about their experiences of workplace discrimination and sexual harassment. Not to mention the testimonies of waitresses, nurses, flight attendants and bartenders whose public-facing jobs present the particular challenge of simultaneous sexual harassment from clients, customers and patients. Or the mechanics, engineers, pilots and plumbers whose working lives are a daily litany of assumptions about their inferiority and requests to 'speak to a man'. Or the women on zero-hours contracts without HR departments to complain to, pressured to put up with sexual harassment because complaining would mean losing their job altogether. Or those part-time workers, often caring for children or dependent parents, whose reduced hours come at the cost of lower wages and zero chance of career advancement.

In 2016, the Everyday Sexism Project and the Trades Union Congress (TUC) published the results of a joint piece of research into the experiences of women in the workplace, the first of its kind undertaken in the UK in over a decade. The representative YouGov survey revealed some shocking truths. Over half of all women, and two-thirds of young women, said they'd experienced workplace sexual harassment. The day the research was released, I did back-to-back interviews, discussing it across the national and regional media. The morning started out well enough, with straightforward segments revealing the findings and interviewers asking for more details. But by early afternoon, the tenor of the coverage was shifting. I was repeatedly asked if I would come on a radio or television programme to 'debate' the results alongside somebody who thought women had it easy in the workplace, or another panellist who believed we should shut up and stop making a fuss. By the evening, I appeared on a national news programme alongside another contributor who was given ample airtime to suggest that women deliberately use their sexuality to get ahead at work and that sexual harassment in the workplace, which she redefined as flirting, was completely natural. To me, this spoke volumes about the level of our societal denial of this particular problem. Rock-solid data about the serious harassment of a group of people in the workplace (revealing, among other things, that one-fifth of women had received unwanted sexual advances and over a tenth unwanted sexual touching) was greeted with dismissal, doubt and disbelief on the national news.

The same phenomenon emerged in the wake of the Harvey Weinstein scandal, after 12 million women worldwide used the hashtag #MeToo to share stories of sexual harassment at work (and elsewhere). The story quickly grew, with women working in Westminster adding their own voices to describe frequent sexual harassment and abuse within politics. But newspapers attempted to belittle the outpouring of experiences by running articles with headlines like: 'A clumsy pass over dinner is NOT sex harassment'. I was invited on the BBC's flagship *Newsnight* programme to discuss the wave of testimonies of rape and assault, only to find the discussion reduced to a debate about whether men were now too afraid to approach women at all, and whether touching a woman's elbow to let her know she had dropped something constituted a form of harassment. On BBC Radio 4's *Today* programme, presenter John Humphrys asked William Hague whether there was a danger that MPs would no longer be able to ask anybody out on a date. In a stunning feat of combined misogyny and Islamophobia, *Daily Mail* columnist Peter Hitchens managed to contort the situation into a column entitled: "What will women gain from all this squawking about sex pests? A niqab". One highly respected TV programme invited me to take part in a 'debate' about the ongoing revelations of abuse against women in the workplace with an email entitled: "Has feminism gone too far?"

The problem doesn't end with sexual harassment. Recent figures from the Equality and Human Rights Commission reveal that a shocking 54,000 women a year are estimated to

lose their jobs as a result of maternity discrimination, representing around one in eight of all pregnant women in the UK.

We tell women to 'lean in', but those who do negotiate
more firmly or act assertively at work are often lambasted and
punished. They're seen as abrasive and shrill where their male
peers would be considered authoritative and ambitious. We
expect women to speak up if they experience discrimination
but many who do are rewarded with a backlash at best, or
redundancy at worst. Little surprise that 80 per cent of women
in the Everyday Sexism and TUC research didn't feel able to
report the sexual harassment to their employer, especially considering the further results that among those who did report,
three-quarters saw no change and 16 per cent said they were
treated worse as a result.

We complain that women simply aren't applying to certain fields in great enough numbers, while presenting girls
with stereotypes and media portrayals that teach them those
fields are not for them. We expect more women to move into
male-dominated industries but those who do often face strato-
spheric levels of harassment and discrimination. We encourage
women to combine motherhood with career, but fire them
for becoming pregnant. And in every field, from the BBC to
Hollywood, the football pitch to the boardroom, we pay them
less than men for the same work. Recent figures revealing
that just a third of the BBC's top earners are women and that
just two of its fourteen top-paid staff were female, as well as
exposing a pay gap for BAME employees, represent the very
tip of the iceberg.

This isn't only devastating for women. When systemic
discrimination renders career opportunities off-limits for

over half the population, every business, organization and workplace suffers. Picking from a pool of only white, male candidates inevitably diminishes the excellence of the workforce by excluding some of the finest prospective workers. Workplace harassment and abuse cost businesses millions in tribunal fees, diminished productivity and lost employees. Studies repeatedly reveal that organizations with better diversity on their boards perform better and flourish financially. Fixing the problem is in everybody's interest.

TEN SEXIST SCENARIOS THAT WOMEN FACE AT WORK

Each of these situations has been reported again and again to the Everyday Sexism Project. For most men, they will be difficult to imagine. For many women, they are painfully familiar.

1. Being mistaken for the secretary

'Although I've been a senior figure in client meetings, when all other attendees are men it's regularly expected that I'm the one to take notes and distribute drinks.'

'I am head of the fundraising department in the charity I work for. Every time I go to a meeting with the man in my department, he is greeted first, his hand is shaken first and the conversation is directed towards him. Once, I was asked if I was there to take notes *even* after I had been introduced as the manager.'

2. Being told to make the tea

'International visitors from the company's head office came for a meeting at which I, the only female in management, had to report. I walked in with my report and they asked for coffee, white with two sugars.'

3. Being called a 'good girl'

'Being told I'm a "good girl" when offering ideas to senior management. Have to resist the urge to bark. A raised eyebrow and "I'm sorry, I didn't quite catch that" worked with one. The other just repeated it . . . I did call one of them a good boy once, but not in a meeting. He seemed to get my point but said that they "didn't mean anything by it".'

4. Being accused of menstruation when voicing a firm opinion

'My colleague had to chase up someone in another department for not meeting a deadline for paperwork to be submitted. When she went to speak with him about it, his response was: "Is it your time of the month?" This is in a huge listed company. She's a lawyer.'

5. Being asked if 'a man is available instead'

'Working in a law office, I've had plenty of people on the phone demand to speak to a man instead of me.'

'People asking if another vicar is available for wedding/ funeral: "Nothing personal but we'd prefer a man."'

6. Having an idea ignored only to be repeated by a male colleague five minutes later to interest and applause

'A female friend of mine in an office meeting proposed a logical, simple solution to a recurring issue. Blank stares from the group and a "We've never done it that way" from the senior (female) manager. A male colleague then makes the exact same suggestion and the room nods enthusiastically and congratulates him on the idea.'

'I attended a meeting last week where a question was posed. I knew the answer and told everybody: "The answer is yes, there is going to be a group assigned to do this." The chair of the meeting (a man) ignored my comment completely and said to everyone: "I think the answer is probably yes, the board promised to work on this topic so I guess they will assign a committee." I shared a look with the only woman in the room, sighed and repeated: "Actually yes, I KNOW there is a committee assigned to this task." I wished this was the first time that this happened . . . it is not.'

7. Being asked about childcare plans

'During my interview for my current position I was asked if I planned on having any more children and what my childcare arrangements are. Each time the question was preceded with: "I'm probably not supposed to ask this but . . ." Too blinking right you're not supposed to ask it! Would you have asked it if I were a male candidate?'

8. Being considered a 'maternity risk'

'I had an interview for an office job for a small company when I was in my early twenties. The senior partner who owned the company told me they wouldn't hire me because I would probably get pregnant and go on maternity leave, and that if I repeated what he'd said he'd deny it.'

9. Being accused of 'baby brain'

'I was told on my first day back [from maternity leave]: "You'll never be the same for us now you have baby brain."'

'I recently came back from maternity leave to my overseas posting, to meet the new boss for the first time. In our first meeting, he explained that I would no longer be in charge of the unit I had been setting up for a year due to my "special circumstances" . . . He also stated that while I was nursing it would be difficult for me to focus on my job, so he was being generous by giving me less responsibility, and downgrading my position.'

10. Avoiding wandering hands

'I was twenty-two, just graduated from university and working a three-month trial period at a very small company – just me and the boss (married, with kids my age). One day I was busy with filing, and the boss came up behind me, wrapped his arms around me and stuck his tongue on my ear. I shoved him away and told him not to do that again. Ended up being fired a week later because I wouldn't have an affair with him.'

If these scenarios sound shocking to the male reader, try running them by some of the women you know – you might be surprised to find how common they are. For many women, this piece will read less like an article and more like a bingo card – how many did you cross off?

Originally published 30 July 2014

FEMALE ACADEMICS FACE HUGE
SEXIST BIAS – NO WONDER
THERE ARE SO FEW OF THEM

Benjamin Schmidt, an assistant professor at Northeastern University, has created an online tool that allows users to compare the frequency of particular words in evaluations of male and female professors. Schmidt created the interactive chart using data from 14 million student reviews on the website RateMyProfessors.com. The results are striking.

We already know that performance evaluations can reveal serious gender bias, whether deliberate or unconscious. But this new data seems to suggest that the problem starts earlier, and is already in full effect during higher education.

There is something almost hypnotic about typing search terms into Schmidt's tool and watching the coloured dots swim from one side of the chart to the other, splitting themselves repeatedly along gender lines. The more terms you can think of, the more the tool reiterates (most) societal stereotypes. Try switching from 'funny' to 'annoying', for example, and watch the dots zoom towards opposite sides of the screen.

Reviews of male professors are more likely to include the words 'brilliant', 'intelligent' or 'smart', and far more likely to contain the word 'genius'. Meanwhile, women are more likely to be described as 'mean', 'harsh', 'unfair' or 'strict', and a lot more likely to be called 'annoying'.

Immediately recognizable societal stereotypes emerge – the words 'disorganized' or 'unorganized' come up much more frequently in women's evaluations, while men are far more likely to be described as 'cool' or 'funny', with one of the widest gender splits of all on the word 'hilarious'. Women are more commonly called 'nice' or 'helpful', but men are more often described as 'good'.

There is a silver lining here – while the results certainly reinforce gender stereotypes about intelligence and personality, there is less focus on female professors' looks than one might anticipate. The search term 'hot' reveals completely mixed results and, though it is used rarely, the word 'sexy' is more likely to appear in evaluations of male rather than female teachers. The battle isn't entirely won, however, as 'beautiful' does crop up for female teachers, albeit far more rarely than other descriptors such as 'good' or 'funny'.

As Schmidt himself points out, the reliability of the data is limited – these are online reviews rather than official student feedback; it's not possible to break down the results by the sex of the reviewer; and, of course, there is room for error in making assumptions about the sentiment of a sentence containing any given word. But this can be mitigated in part by Schmidt's tool, which allows users to see the frequency of each word (with higher frequency results likely to be more reliable), and to filter for results from only positive or negative evaluations.

The findings are also backed up by other studies, one of which surveyed college students' feedback about online course professors and found that the ratings were higher in every category when students were told the professor was male. The strength of this unconscious bias is quite astonishing – even for a relatively objective measure such as promptness, students rated a 'female' professor 3.55 out of 5 and a 'male' professor 4.35, despite the fact that they handed work back at the same time.

The implications are serious. In the competitive world of academia, student evaluations are often used as a tool in the process of hiring and promotion. That the evaluations may be biased against female professors is particularly problematic in light of existing gender imbalance, particularly at the highest echelons of academia. According to the American Association of University Professors, in 2012, 62 per cent of men in academia in the US were tenured compared to only 44 per cent of women, while women were far more likely to be in non-tenure track positions than men (32 per cent of women in academia compared to just 19 per cent of men).

Meanwhile, statistics obtained in 2013 by Times Higher Education revealed that only about one in five UK professors are female, with the percentage of female professors at some universities as low as 8 or 9 per cent. Data from the non-profit organization Catalyst suggests that the imbalance persists internationally, too.

Set alongside the unconscious bias of academic recruiters themselves, as well as the difficulty of juggling parenthood with the demands of research, the apparent sexism in student evaluations provides yet another hurdle for women in academia.

It is interesting to consider these results in the context of a wave of troubling recent reports about sexism and misogyny on campus. Perhaps it will be difficult to tackle biased and sexist appraisals of female professors until the wider issue of student sexism is also seriously confronted.

Originally published 13 February 2015

TEN THINGS YOU SHOULD KNOW ABOUT THE GENDER PAY GAP

According to the Fawcett Society, 9 November marked Equal Pay Day – the date from which women in Britain effectively work for free until the end of the year, due to the 14.2 per cent gender pay gap. Myths and misconceptions still persist around unequal pay. (This week alone I've heard 'the gender pay gap doesn't exist', 'women shouldn't have babies if they're going to complain' and 'women aren't paid less, they just *earn* less'.) So in the interests of clearing up some confusion, here are ten facts you might not know about the pay gap . . .

1. It starts young . . . really young

A website set up to allow parents to pay pocket money to their children via online accounts revealed that boys were paid 15 per cent more than girls for doing the same chores. The gap widened for homework, where boys received more than double the amount of pocket money girls did for completing an assignment.

2. It's an intersectional problem

Research by Race for Opportunity found that black, Asian and minority ethnic (BAME) workers make up a disproportionate number of people in low-paid jobs, with almost a quarter (23 per cent) of Pakistani employees and a fifth of Bangladeshi, Chinese and Black Caribbean workers earning less than £25,000 per year. It also found that a white British employee has an average of almost four promotions during their career, compared to just 2.5 for British African, Indian and Pakistani employees. Figures from the Low Pay Commission found that 15.3 per cent of Pakistani/Bangladeshi workers earned the minimum wage – more than twice the number of white workers in minimum wage jobs. Teach First research has revealed that young people from disadvantaged backgrounds are paid 10 per cent less than peers with the same qualifications, even after graduating from university. And the pay gap is wider for older women than for their younger colleagues, with women in their fifties earning nearly a fifth less than men of the same age.

Research also suggests that trans women are more economically vulnerable and can earn almost a third less after transitioning.

3. It's complicated

The pay gap exists for many and complex reasons. As well as both direct and indirect discrimination, there are issues such as occupational segregation and the devaluation of jobs primarily associated with female labour. The fact that women make up the majority of part-time and low-paid workers, and the relative lack of promotion opportunities for part-time workers, are also factors. Among part-time workers, women are still more likely to be lower paid than men.

4. It happens across a huge variety of professions

Attention has recently been drawn to the wage gap between male and female stars in Hollywood. But the gender pay gap affects everybody from architects to athletes. Recent research from the Office for National Statistics revealed that female architects are paid a whopping 25 per cent less than their male counterparts. And while members of the England women's football team earn around £20,000 per year, male Premier League players earn an average of £1.6 million per year.

5. It's not performance-based

Talking of football, the US national teams recently provided a stunning, high-profile example of pay failing to correlate to performance. In the World Cup, the women's team were victorious, winning the whole championship, while the men's team went out in the first round. But the women's team won prize money of $2 million, while the men won $8 million just for being eliminated at the first hurdle.

6. While working mothers lose out, working fathers actually benefit

We all know that the motherhood penalty can have a huge negative impact on women's careers. Mothers are less likely to get jobs in the first place, and less likely to be paid as well as their similarly qualified male colleagues. But to add insult to injury, working fathers actually see a boost to their salaries, with their earnings increasing an average of over 6 per cent when they have children, compared to mothers, whose salaries decrease 4 per cent for each child on average.

7. It affects graduates too

Much has been made recently of the diminishing pay gap among younger workers. But studies still show a graduate pay gap, where women can earn up to £8,000 less in their starting salaries than their male peers who took the same degree.

According to the Higher Education Careers Service Unit, one in five men are paid more than £30,000 after their degree, compared with just 8 per cent of women who earn the same. And research from the Higher Education Statistics Agency found that the average graduate salary is £2,000 higher for male graduates than for female graduates.

8. Not all work 'counts'

As Katrine Marçal points out in her recent book, *Who Cooked Adam Smith's Dinner?*, the very methods by which we measure and value labour have long disregarded the enormous contribution and impact of the unpaid domestic and caring work carried out predominantly by women.

9. It can arise from subtle bias

When we think of the pay gap, it's easy to imagine a villainous boss deliberately choosing to pay a female employee less than her male counterparts. But while that can happen, discrimination can also be more complex. A study published in the journal *Proceedings of the National Academy of Sciences* submitted identical applications for laboratory manager jobs, but assigned female-sounding names to half the applications and male-sounding names to the other half. In a randomized double-blind study, participants not only considered the 'male' applicants more competent and hireable, but were also likely to offer them a higher starting salary.

10. Even technology isn't immune from discriminatory practices

It was recently revealed that Google's algorithm displays far fewer adverts for high-paying job opportunities to women than it does to men.

So the next time someone tries to tell you feminism is unnecessary and the gender pay gap doesn't exist, fix them with a beady stare, talk them through its complexities and, if all else fails, hit them with Twitter user @LauraLuchador's viral joke: 'If I had a pound for every time I was told I didn't need feminism I'd have 85p each time.'

Originally published 10 November 2015

HARASSED BY YOUR BOSS AT THE CHRISTMAS PARTY? YOU'RE NOT ALONE

Cornered by lecherous co-workers with wandering hands. Told loudly by a senior colleague that you're too 'hot' to be part of the technical team. Proclaimed winner of the 'best arse' award. Asked 'Shall we just shag?' four times, despite the advances clearly being unwelcome. Offered a colleague a lift home only to be sexually assaulted in the back of a taxi. Alongside the obvious connections, these experiences have one thing in common that might surprise you. They all happened to women attending work Christmas parties.

Around this time of year, the Everyday Sexism Project sees an upsetting spike in stories from working women who have experienced sexism, harassment and even assault at annual company festivities. The stories are varied and complex. In some cases, women are excluded from the party altogether, missing out on networking opportunities and sidelined from the team:

'I'm a female working in the construction industry. Currently, I and one other female work here, and neither of us are invited to the Christmas party. I've worked here for four years and I've never been invited (in my first year I was invited and then uninvited because it might be "awkward"). We've kicked up a bit a fuss this year, but my boss will not let us come because "it has been this way for years".'

Many examples (such as being sexually propositioned by married colleagues) assume an atmosphere of conspiratorial 'naughtiness' at such events. Some reports amount to sexual assault:

'My boss's boss, a married man, made several attempts to molest me at a Christmas party, including grabbing my breasts, pulling me towards him, slapping my bottom and trying to force unwanted kisses on me. Exasperated, I eventually told him to "fuck off", then spent an anxious weekend worrying that I would lose my job. Fortunately, I didn't, but he continued pestering me. Everyone thought it was funny and that I should be flattered.'

Others demonstrate how a culture of complicity and normalization can prevent perpetrators from facing any ramifications: 'One of the men in my office chased one of the women into a room at the Christmas party and wouldn't let her leave until she kissed him. Everyone knows he did it. He's still considered a "nice guy".'

While some argue that this is 'no big deal', the long-term impact is often much greater than one might realize: 'While working for a law firm and attending the Christmas party, one of the male partners told me that my dress was pretty, but would look better crumpled on his bedroom floor. He kept asking to walk me home, even though he was married and I was living with my boyfriend at the time. I felt quite frightened of him and left the party swiftly when he wasn't looking so I could get home without the fear of being pursued. I complained to my boss who, of course, had a word with him, but he continued to make my working life intolerable, so I left.'

For many women who experience a surge of workplace harassment in environments such as restaurants and bars ('I'm dressed as Santa, sit on my lap'; 'Have you been naughty or nice?'; 'Give us a Christmas kiss'), there isn't necessarily an HR department to notify, nor a means of complaining without jeopardizing what might already be an uncontracted and low-paid position. For those dependent on tips, with the directive to keep customers happy, handling harassment becomes even more difficult.

The only way to solve this problem for all workers, not just those who are in a strong enough position to protest, is to demand that workplaces tackle the issue at the source. This is not as difficult as some make out. If we expect employers to protect employees from sexual harassment in the workplace, they should maintain the same basic standards at festive events – indeed, according to the law, they must.

Many elements of the problem (inviting only male employees; holding the party in a strip club; giving out inappropriate rewards) are within the organizers' control. Others, such as inappropriate behaviour, should be tackled with clear zero-tolerance policies and transparent, protected reporting procedures.

It's a red herring to suggest, as many people do, that cracking down on sexual harassment will create an awkward atmosphere or take the fun out of the office Christmas party. Being the target of sexist jokes or groping on the dancefloor is what prevents many employees from having fun in the first place.

Originally published 22 December 2015

WHY DO SO FEW SERVICEWOMEN REPORT EXPERIENCES OF SEXUAL HARASSMENT?

In 2011, it was estimated that a female soldier serving in Iraq was more likely to be attacked by a fellow soldier than killed by enemy fire. The problems of rape, sexual assault and sexual harassment in the military are not new, but in recent years there has been an increase in attention to these issues, resulting in greater efforts being made to tackle them, particularly in the US military.

Now, a new army-commissioned survey has revealed that levels of sexual harassment in the British army are worryingly high. The survey of 7,000 soldiers found that almost 40 per cent of servicewomen said they had received unwanted comments of a sexual nature in the past year alone. Of the women surveyed, 39 per cent said they had received unwelcome comments about their appearance, body or sexual activities. And 33 per cent said that someone had made unwelcome attempts to talk to them about sexual matters. In some cases, the harassment escalated to physical assault, with 12 per cent of women surveyed saying that someone had made unwelcome attempts to touch them. Around one-fifth of men also reported unwanted comments about their appearance, body or sexual activities.

Army chief General Sir Nick Carter described the levels of sexual harassment as 'totally unacceptable', saying he was 'disappointed by the figures'.

Since the Everyday Sexism Project was launched in 2012 to catalogue experiences of gender inequality, many women have posted about their experiences in the military: from subtle sexism, to more aggressive harassment, to assault.

One servicewoman wrote: 'The army is working hard to stamp out sexism but some seniors still set a bad example. Every time my company parades, the Sergeant Major addresses the parade as "Gentlemen" despite there being half a dozen women in the company. Also, when there are social events we are told we may invite wives or girlfriends; husbands and boyfriends are never mentioned.'

Another said: 'When I was in the army, the other guys referred to the only female soldier in our company as a "field mattress" who had only joined the army because she was "too ugly to get any cock" in any arena where the guys had other options. Incidentally, she finished first in the company's 30 km march.'

One woman's entry read: 'I was touched without permission while on guard at night in Iraq, with a loaded weapon. In my report I wrote that I had considered using my rifle should the male have gone any further and [I] was reprimanded for this.'

Entries suggest that the problem is by no means confined to the army, nor just to the UK, with servicewomen from other branches of the military and from around the world also sharing their stories.

One woman wrote: 'I'm a US marine, so you can imagine the barrage of sexism I deal with. Men think it's okay to slap you on your ass when you're in charge of them.'

Entries range from low-level sexism to more severe offences. One reads: 'I joined the navy at sixteen. During basic training I was forced to have sex with a physical training instructor; he told me I wouldn't pass my course unless I did. He used the same bribe to make me perform a sex act on him . . . The entire episode was swept under the carpet. After leaving basic training to commence trade training as an engineer, I was the youngest and only female in my class. The men laid bets on who could sleep with me first. It took me a while to figure out why they were being so nice.'

Many women also described how sexism can interfere with their ability to carry out their jobs: 'I was in training, leading a combined infantry and armoured company rolling attack over three objectives. The armoured commander wouldn't take orders from me on the radio because I am a girl.'

The British army survey suggests that reporting rates are woefully low, with only about 3 per cent of those service-women who were 'very upset' about an incident of sexual harassment making a formal written complaint. This is also borne out by the accounts submitted to Everyday Sexism, with many women apparently choosing not to report incidents because of the fear of being disbelieved, or marked out as a 'troublemaker': 'One of my sergeants when I was deployed liked to grab at me . . . my butt, my thighs, or accidentally "touch" my breasts. I reported it to higher, like I was told. I expected a change. I expected something to be done . . . I was alienated. Most of my fellow soldiers would not talk to ME anymore: not my groping sergeant, me! The other females he was touching refused to come forward after they saw how I was treated. No one wants to be around the "tattletale".'

The good news is that the issue is finally starting to receive the attention – and action – it deserves. General Carter told the BBC that while he was disappointed with the survey results, 'they do provide me with a baseline from which I can move forward and change the army's culture'.

He follows in the footsteps of Lieutenant General David Morrison, former chief of the Australian army, whose rousing speech and tough rhetoric about unacceptable behaviour in the Australian army went viral in 2013. Such top-down leadership will be vital to challenge an ingrained culture of sexual harassment, particularly in a traditionally male-dominated institution like the army.

Finally, the project entries also make it clear that in order to fully support our servicewomen, we need to see a shift in attitudes outside the military too:

'Response after telling people we're a military family: they turn to my husband and thank him for his service.'

Originally published 14 July 2015

THE HOTLY CONTESTED OLYMPIC
MEDAL TABLE OF SEXISM

If sexism were an Olympic sport, the competition would be very tough indeed. Over the past two weeks, hopefuls from across the media have battled it out against some of the greatest in the world. Many have been in training for years. For others, it was their first foray into the competition. Not everybody can go home with a medal, but as the games draw to a close, here's a round-up of the most decorated contenders . . .

Most tired gender stereotype

Bronze medal
Al Trautwig, who speculated that Dutch gymnast Sanne Wevers might be writing a 'dear diary' entry when she was seen jotting something down after completing her routine – she was in fact working out her scores.

Silver medal
The BBC commentator who described a women's Olympic judo match as a 'catfight'.

Gold medal
Jim Watson, who observed the USA women's gymnastics team conferring on the sidelines and mused: 'They might as well be standing around at the mall.'

Most irrelevant commentary on women's appearance

Bronze medal

The *Daily Mail*'s 'best dressed' list, comparing the outfits of female sports reporters.

Silver medal

Jointly awarded to every outraged and gleeful article about BBC commentator Helen Skelton's legs.

Gold medal

The detailed commentary setting female gymnasts up against one another and reducing them entirely to their leotards, including references to how 'dainty' or 'ultra-feminine' they were and even comparing them to Disney fairies. Criticisms included the accusation that one gymnast 'turned heads for all the wrong reasons' and even that one leotard didn't 'complement' the gymnast's skin tone.

Most insulting attribution of a female athlete's medal to her husband

Silver medal

The *Chicago Tribune*, for its Twitter headline: 'Wife of a Bears' lineman wins a bronze medal today in Rio Olympics'.

Gold medal

Commentator Dan Hicks, who was reporting on the women's 400 m individual medley in swimming when Hungary's Katinka Hosszú took the gold medal and beat the existing world record by over two seconds. As the camera panned over to her husband and coach in the stands, Hicks told viewers: 'And there's the man responsible.'

Most blatant prioritizing of men's achievements over women's

Silver medal

The headline that relegated Katie Ledecky's record-breaking gold medal win to a small-print subtitle beneath news of Michael Phelps tying for silver in the 100 m fly.

Gold medal

The dehumanizing headline that failed even to name swimmer Simone Manuel after she won a gold medal in the 100 m freestyle. Instead the tweeted headline ran: 'Olympics: Michael Phelps shares historic night with African-American'.

Most enormous double standard

Silver medal

The reaction of outrage and abuse when US gymnast Gabby Douglas failed to put her hand over her heart during the national anthem, while Michael Phelps got off far more lightly for laughing on the podium during the anthem.

Gold medal

The TV-viewing public who were scandalized when they thought they caught the briefest glimpse of Helen Skelton's underwear as she reported from the hot and humid aquatics centre ... but later complained that Gary Lineker didn't flash enough flesh when he presented *Match of the Day* in his underwear.

Most egregious all-round sexism

Bronze medal

Jointly awarded to all the commentators who contributed to the sexist bias in the language used about female Olympians. According to researchers at Cambridge University Press, while language like 'fastest', 'strongest', 'biggest' was commonly used to describe male athletes, female athletes attracted words like 'married' and 'unmarried', as well as references to their age.

Silver medal

NBC executive John Miller, who responded to complaints about frequent ad breaks and interruptions in the Olympic coverage by saying: 'The people who watch the Olympics are not particularly sports fans. More women watch the games than men, and for the women, they're less interested in the result and more interested in the journey. It's sort of like the ultimate reality show and miniseries wrapped into one.'

Gold medal

The Fox News segment that saw two male commentators discuss female Olympians' appearance. One said: 'Why should I have to look at some chick's zits?'

And, because we all need something to cheer for . . .

Best comeback to sexism

Gold medal

Simone Biles, who had the perfect comeback after commentators kept comparing her with great male athletes. After her outstanding performance, which saw her win five medals, Biles said: 'I'm not the next Usain Bolt or Michael Phelps. I'm the first Simone Biles.'

Though these lucky winners go home with medals, they only represent the tip of the iceberg. Here's hoping we don't see any of these categories being contested in Tokyo in 2020.

Originally published 22 August 2016

SEXUAL HARASSMENT IN THE WORKPLACE IS ENDEMIC

'Was asked to join in threesome with boss and his deputy' . . . 'Told to sit on my boss's lap if I wanted my Christmas bonus' . . . 'Heard partners assessing female candidates according to their attractiveness' . . . 'Told to get an abortion or resign as two pregnant workers was unfair' . . .

Workplace harassment is one of the most common issues reported to the Everyday Sexism Project – in fact, we have collected nearly 10,000 entries on this topic alone.

So it is no surprise today that a new study by law firm Slater & Gordon has revealed that one in six women have had colleagues look down their blouse, almost half have experienced comments about their breasts in the workplace and one in eight have left jobs because workplace harassment made them feel so uncomfortable. The study suggests that sexual harassment in the workplace is rife among both men and women, with almost 40 per cent of men also reporting experiences. But 60 per cent of those surveyed say they have kept a possible harassment incident to themselves, making this an invisible yet enormously common problem. Indeed, the experiences quoted throughout this article have all been reported to the Everyday Sexism Project in the past eighteen months alone.

Workplace sexual harassment is one of the most difficult and insidious issues to tackle because victims are so often in a position of vulnerability, afraid of damaging their careers or even losing their jobs altogether if they dare to rock the boat:

'When I was twenty-three my arse was regularly pinched at work. I was too afraid of losing my job to report it.'

'I work in a bar and face constant, ongoing, never-ending abuse from men ordering drinks ... I know if I complained I'd have to leave my job.'

Perpetrators are often much older and more experienced than their victims, and in many cases are even in a position of responsibility over them, making it near-impossible for those being harassed to complain:

'Had a manager that said he would "totally rape me".'

'A guy at my work told me he'd get me fired if I didn't have sex with him. His brother was the boss.'

What's worse is that even when victims do find the courage to come forward, they frequently report being dismissed, as the problem is belittled and normalized:

'A male boss said he'd "love to bend me over" and more, I reported it to female supervisor who said I was being "sensitive".'

'Saw my hours cut every time I complained to a manager about the co-worker who sexually harassed me and then threatened me.'

Part of the problem is that the sorts of issues reported in the Slater & Gordon study, including having your bottom pinched, are widely considered 'just a bit of fun', making it hard for workers to feel able to speak out against them:

'When a customer at work tried to reach his hand down my shirt, I wasn't taken seriously by any of my co-workers.'

Often, there is a sense that everybody is 'in on the joke', so victims feel unable to speak up for fear of being branded humourless, or a troublemaker: 'While I was bending over to pick up stock, male colleague grabbed my hips & simulated sex. Everyone else laughed.'

The irony is that while such experiences are tolerated and brushed under the carpet due to normalization and a culture of acceptance, in fact everybody is legally protected from sexual harassment in the UK workplace, including protection against the violation of a person's dignity or the creation of an intimidating, hostile, degrading, humiliating or offensive environment. Almost every one of the thousands of incidents reported to us would fall under these categories, yet again and again victims say they feel unable to speak up for fear of not being taken seriously or of losing their jobs.

Part of the reason for this, just as with so many other forms of harassment and assault, is victim-blaming. When workplace harassment hits the headlines, people often react by asking why victims don't simply stand up for themselves – why didn't they make a fuss or firmly put their harasser in his or her place? This attitude completely fails to take into account the power dynamics of many workplace harassment scenarios; the vulnerability of many victims and the fear of losing one's job, particularly at a time when employment is scarce and public attitudes towards victims are unsympathetic. Even if some people are able to stand up for themselves in such a scenario, the point is that nobody should have to – these are serious offences, protected against by law, and they should be treated as such.

The entries we are receiving day in, day out, clearly indicate that the problem has reached epidemic proportions:

'There will be at least three shifts a week at work where I am spanked, grabbed, groped or stroked.'

'As junior doctor, asked consultant for second opinion on an X-ray. "Only if you sit on my lap while we look at it."'

'A boss once cornered me in office after everyone left, told me wouldn't let me leave until I agreed to go out with him. I was sixteen.'

It's time to start taking workplace harassment seriously, listening to victims and, above all, placing blame firmly where it belongs: with the perpetrator.

Originally published 23 October 2013

FACEPALM FAILS

Every now and then an idea comes along that is so utterly stupid, crass or insensitive that it is impossible to believe it was waved through what must have been several stages of sign-offs and approvals. Into this category fall examples like the 'Bic for her', a pen designed especially for the fragile female hand; the UK government decision to force women to pay for their own rape crisis services using proceeds from the tampon tax; and the Cardiff buses advertised using a picture of a naked woman and the slogan 'Ride me all day for £3'. The FA gets an honourable mention for its tweet welcoming home the bronze medal-winning women's World Cup team with a message that began: "Our #Lionesses go back to being mothers, partners and daughters today . . ." In fact, I could go on and on.

What's most shocking about these facepalm-worthy fails is that they aren't accidental. People have sat down together around a meeting table somewhere and said 'Hey, this seems like a great plan!' And at no point from the initial idea to its execution has any policymaker, company boss or stakeholder said 'Hang on a second, there might just be something a tad . . .

sexist about that.' In fact, in most cases, they clearly thought they were on to an absolutely brilliant idea.

That is perhaps the most eye-opening aspect of these examples. They don't only reveal the extent of ingrained sexism in our society, but the widespread lack of awareness of the problem. Even when people are actively thinking about initiatives to engage women and girls in areas where they are traditionally under-represented, they don't see a problem with using sexism and stereotypes to try to address the gap. The irony is astounding.

WHY 'ENGINEERING BARBIE'S' PINK WASHING MACHINE DEFEATS THE POINT

'Math class is tough,' declared Barbie in 1992, prompting a backlash from the American Association of University Women and a swift adjustment to the toy's verbal repertoire. It wasn't the first time the unrealistically proportioned doll had attracted criticisms of sexism, and it wouldn't be the last. Barbie Babysitter came with a book entitled *How to Lose Weight*, which contained the helpful advice: 'Don't eat.' And Slumber Party Barbie was supplied with a set of pink scales fixed at 110 lb (50 kg) – 35 lb underweight for her supposed 5 ft 9 in frame.

In 2010, a Barbie book titled *I Can Be a Computer Engineer* clearly had good intentions, but attracted derision after suggesting that Barbie couldn't achieve technological success without the help of male friends. (After she crashed two laptops, the boys took over, telling her: 'Step aside, Barbie. YOU'VE BROKEN ENOUGH, NOW.') Barbie manufacturer Mattel apologized and withdrew the book from online sale.

So you might think that by 2017, following a recent relaunch supposedly aimed at bringing Barbie into the twenty-first century with more varied body sizes and skin tones, important lessons about stereotyping and sexism might finally have been learned. Apparently not.

Step forward Engineering Barbie, a doll designed to encourage girls into a field in which women are enormously under-represented. So far, so good. Except the products that

Engineering Barbie encourages girls to build are limited almost entirely to the realm of fashion and household chores: dresses, a moving clothes rack and a washing machine. And, yes, they are all pink. Created by toy company Thames and Kosmos, the Barbie STEM kit also offers girls aged from four to eight the opportunity to build a jewellery holder and a shoe rack.

The contradictory messaging, which sets out with the aim of overcoming gender stereotypes before falling for them hook, line and sinker, is just the latest in a long line of very similar failures. The European Commission's doomed 'Science: it's a girl thing!' campaign tried to excite girls about chemistry with a pink lipstick logo and a video featuring giggling, mini-skirted girls dancing amid floating make-up. Then there was energy company EDF's misguidedly named #PrettyCurious campaign, swiftly followed by IBM's #HackAHairdryer.

How does this keep on happening? Who has enough aware-ness of these issues to sit in a production meeting and discuss the need for more progressive toys, but then *doesn't* have the awareness to add: 'Maybe it shouldn't be pink and deal solely with domestic chores because that defeats the entire point'?

There's really only one conceivable explanation: people still don't see the problem with directing hugely stereotyped, patronizing and limited messaging towards girls and young women. There remains a widespread consensus that the way to attract girls to a male-dominated field is to focus on hearts, cupcakes and high heels. While recent attempts, such as Engineering Barbie, represent a major step forward in recog-nizing that action is needed to tackle the under-representation of girls in science, technology and engineering, it's ridiculous to think that the solution lies in perpetuating the very stereotypes that are partially responsible for the problem in the first place.

Luckily, there are some good examples out there, from Lammily, the doll with acne, stretch marks and cellulite, to Roominate, a range of building and engineering toys aimed at girls. Online resources such as coding websites and apps for kids and the Science Museum's online games also provide great starting points for parents who want to expose girls to science and computing.

The more these sexist mistakes pile up, the harder it is to excuse the next misguided campaign. It's surely not rocket science to realize that if we want to attract more girls to STEM, we need to ditch the stereotypes.

Originally published 26 January 2017

HOW CAN WE BEAT SEXISM IN FOOTBALL? PINK WHISTLES AT THE READY!

The Football Association has revealed its innovative ideas for attracting more girls into the sport, which include pink whistles, nice-smelling bibs and allowing girls breaks to stop and check their phones.

The plan, hosted on the Sussex FA website, also advises advertising 'in places where girls go', such as 'coffee shops or the backs of toilet doors', and suggests using discount clothes vouchers as an incentive. Possible slogans to attract girls include: 'You won't even notice you're getting fit!' and 'Who needs Facebook friends?'

While the drive to think about making the sport more accessible to women is welcome, some young female football fans have already made their thoughts on the list clear, writing to let the FA know that 'we aren't all brainless Barbie dolls'.

As the debate continues, how about similar guidelines for helping women and girls get ahead in other tricky, male-dominated areas?

Getting women into politics

- Insert small cosmetic mirrors along the back of each bench in the House of Commons.
- Slip a discreet handbag-sized brochure of eligible male MPs into the graduation packs of female politics students.
- Encourage even more media coverage of the great shoes female MPs get the chance to wear.

- Suggested slogan: 'You might be told to "Calm down, dear", but it's the taking part that counts!'

... and business

- Scented toilet paper in the company lavatories.
- Replace office Christmas tree decorations with miniature tampons.
- Launch an all-female office snowboarding trip so the organization can technically claim higher numbers of 'women on boards'.
- Suggested slogan: 'You'll be having so much fun you won't even notice you're being paid 15 per cent less!'

... science

- More competitions about make-up and hairdryers. They've worked so well in the past!
- Nice-smelling lab coats.
- Run a blind-date night where each girl has to come as a different element of the periodic table and find another attractive element to make a compound with.
- Free tissues in the lab for when they start crying everywhere.
- Suggested slogan: 'Science: it's really just all about perfume!'

... engineering

- Create glittery tools that female engineers can buy for a bargain 150 per cent more than the mainstream versions.

- Specifically advertise roles where hairstyle isn't likely to be affected by working conditions (and similar perks).
- Target potential recruits in places where women go, such as Topshop and *Bridget Jones's Baby* screenings.
- Suggested slogan: 'We're only 9 per cent of the workforce and that's before we get pushed out by sexism, but by golly our hair looks good!'

... space

- Astronaut suits with built-in feather boas.
- Free manicures to be performed by male colleagues during re-entry to Earth's atmosphere, in preparation for media coverage on landing.
- A small but well-stocked shoe shop on board the International Space Station.
- Curvier, more feminine-shaped rockets.
- Suggested slogan: 'There's no washing-up to do in space!'

... maths

- Calculator displays that show flowers instead of numbers.
- Seat girls next to male students in the classroom so they can easily learn by peeking at the boys' answers.
- More exam questions about working out VAT on chocolate and the rising price of women's underwear.
- Suggested slogan: 'It's as easy as one, two ... ooh, a pretty flower!'

... tech

- Raise girls' aspirations by increasing the breast size of female characters in computer games just a notch more.
- Distract attention from sexual harassment at conferences using flashing lights and loud music.
- Create some kind of international online mob that can shut down any women who mention sexism in gaming, thus making women feel much safer and attracting them to the industry in hordes.
- Suggested slogan: 'Equal opportunities means women can be harassed in virtual reality too!'

Of course, increasing funding and media coverage for some of our excellent women's football teams might arguably be a good way to encourage girls into the sport. But where's the feminine fun in that?

Originally published 12 December 2016

WHY SHOULD WOMEN HAVE TO PAY THE PRICE FOR 'SAFETY' ON A DAILY BASIS?

Scrolling through my social media feed this morning, I came across a picture of a jagged, dagger-like implement mounted on a plastic ring. It was being recommended as the perfect product for female runners. It is, of course, bright pink. The idea – according to Fisher Defensive, the company behind the Go Guarded self-defence ring – is that 'it is a convenient, comfortable, effective way for women to defend themselves if the unthinkable should happen when they are out running, hiking or walking'.

Convenient? That a product intended as a weapon to fight off sexual assault can be described as 'convenient and comfortable' crystallizes just how blasé we have become about the idea that constant vigilance is a routine part of a woman's reality. It is quite normal to come across products like this. Rape alarms. Pepper spray substitutes. Anti-rape underwear. Anti-Rohypnol nail polish. Anything to remind me to step up, open my wallet and pay the price for 'safety' as a woman in a man's world.

The idea that I need reminding to take extra precautions to try to protect myself is laughable. Women do this every day, in hundreds of tiny ways. For most of us, it is automatic. When you've been shouted at, grabbed and made to feel afraid for your safety by men in the street a hundred times, responses such as crossing the street, doubling back, avoiding darker routes, clenching your fists, walking faster, and countless others, happen instinctively. It still doesn't stop us from being harassed, assaulted and raped.

The reality of how heavily the threat of sexual violence hangs over women's daily lives was laid bare today in new data from ActionAid UK. A poll of 2,200 people revealed that in the past month alone, 57 per cent of British women have experienced some form of harassment and just under one in six (16 per cent) have been groped.

These are shocking statistics. But even more dispiriting is the finding that over 70 per cent of all British women and 88 per cent of those aged 18–24 have taken steps in their everyday lives to guard against harassment. Sexual violence doesn't only impact women's lives in the moment of an assault or an incident of harassment. It affects us every day, influencing our behaviour, our travel plans and our peace of mind.

The poll listed ten different strategies women use to try to avoid harassment, from steering clear of parks or public transport to taking a chaperone or even failing to attend work, school or college altogether. A quarter of the women polled had changed their travel route and 28 per cent had prepared to use an everyday object, such as keys or an umbrella, as a weapon.

We must confront the idea that it is acceptable, normal even, to live in a world where women disrupt their lives to avoid sexual harassment and violence on a daily basis. We must recognize the absurdity and horror of a woman posting a review on the Amazon page for the 'self-defence ring' that reads: 'I still have a small knife in my runner's pocket, but I like the extra time that Go Guarded buys me before pulling out my knife.'

While we are repeatedly told to stop making a fuss because women are equal now, we are buying back-up self-defence weapons to give us time to reach our regular ones. The disparity between the notion that the problem is solved and the toll it takes on women and girls is absurd. So take a step in the opposite direction. Disrupt a norm. Listen to a woman in your life about her experiences of harassment. Talk to your son about sexual consent. Discuss sexual violence with men. And, above all, recognize that this is a reality women live with day in, day out, and it is one that won't be fixed with a bright-pink ring.

Originally published 25 November 2016

STRIPPING MISS GREAT BRITAIN OF HER TITLE FOR HAVING SEX ON TV REVEALS OUR DOUBLE STANDARDS

Miss Great Britain Zara Holland has been stripped of her title after having sex with fellow contestant Alex Bowen on ITV2 reality show *Love Island.*

The official Miss Great Britain Twitter account released a statement saying that the decision had been taken with 'great regret', adding: 'We pride ourselves on promoting the positivity of pageants in modern society and this includes the promotion of a strong, positive female role model in our winners ... The feedback we have received from pageant insiders and members of the general public is such that we cannot promote Zara as a positive role model moving forward ... We wholly understand that everyone makes mistakes, but Zara, as an ambassador for Miss Great Britain, simply did not uphold the responsibility expected of the title.'

As if Holland hasn't already suffered enough after spending the past two weeks stuck on an island with a bunch of sexist men talking about 'leathering' the female contestants and boasting of 'letting' their girlfriends out so other men could admire them before taking them home. Now she has been hung out to dry by a group that has collectively dissected her sexual behaviour and found it wanting, publicly describing her decision to sleep with Bowen on the show as a 'mistake'.

After facing a backlash from Twitter users accusing the pageant of sexism and slut-shaming the 20-year-old, the account tweeted: 'To be clear we have no problem at all with sex – it is perfectly natural. We simply can't condone what happened on national TV.'

Thus, Miss Great Britain provided a fascinating insight into the outdated double standards ingrained into the modern beauty pageant.

In fairness, the organizers of Miss Great Britain aren't entirely ignorant of how archaic the pageant is; their website enthusiastically reminds readers that the first-ever winner won seven guineas and a swimsuit, in an exercise designed so that 'men could enjoy watching pretty girls'. A quick glance at the 2013 finalists photograph on the website suggests that very little has changed: identikit women are lined up like cattle, with identification numbers to boot.

An organization that judges women on how sexy, thin and attractive they are to men has publicly humiliated and degraded its own winner for going on a television programme all about being sexy, thin and attractive to men. When these women are passive objects, the pageant revels in and profits from their sexual attractiveness. But heaven forbid they should actually live a real life or follow through on that titillating promise. The idea of them taking ownership of their own bodies and desires is apparently unthinkable, unless it is done in secret.

It all plays into the double standard that sees young women facing enormous pressure to be as sexy as possible, yet lambasted if they dare to step outside the realm of the watched object and into the role of the self-possessed woman. Looking attractive is all well and good, but dare to engage in actual sexual activity and suddenly you're a slut, a slag, a whore, while your male peers mysteriously become studs, lads or players. It is often the court of public opinion that disgraces and shames women for sexual activity: a pattern replicated in the Miss Great Britain statement, which makes it clear that it is only after receiving feedback that they decided Holland could not be promoted as a role model – a decision based on other people's judgements rather than her own actions.

The move is particularly ironic given that the pageant only recently updated its rules to allow married women and mothers to take part (they were banned from entering until 2013). So having had sex in the past is clearly acceptable, just not in the future.

Of course, Miss Great Britain isn't alone in its double standards – they were also on full display on Love Island itself, where fellow contestants described Holland as an 'absolute idiot' and a 'stupid girl', while Bowen was reported to have escaped 'unscathed by scandal'. In this case, as in so many, others benefitted richly from a young woman being torn down: ratings rocketed after Holland was dethroned.

Stripping Holland of her title is further proof that no matter how hard women try to play by society's sexist rules, they still can't win.

Originally published 21 June 2016

Shouting Back

Often, an interviewer will ask me to name a woman who inspires me. They expect, I think, to hear famous names. But whenever I am asked that question, I immediately think of names that are unlikely to be known to the general public. Names like Rowan Miller. Or Seyi Akiwowo. Or Ellie Cosgrave. These are not famed media figures. They are not being showered with awards. They are unsung heroes. Women at the coalface – women who are working tirelessly, often thanklessly, day after day, to make the world better for other women in their own unique ways. That might mean, respectively, running a regional sexual assault support service, fighting against a wave of vile racist and misogynistic threats to represent their community as a councillor and campaigner, or working tirelessly as an academic to support other women in science and engineering.

I am inspired by the grit and determination of the women who dedicate their lives to making other women's lives better. The Rape Crisis staffers whose professional lives are an endless cycle of uncertainty as they scramble to find next year's budget from an ever-shrinking pot of public funds. The charity workers who face heckling and abuse as they raise their voices about new inequality research or point out the unpopular reality of the crisis in refuge provision or social housing. The campaigners who dedicate their own lives, unpaid and un-thanked, to fighting for the rights of refugee women and those in detention. The clinic escorts who endure threats and loathing to support women exercising their right to reproductive healthcare.

I draw strength, too, from the hordes of people speaking out about these issues in their daily lives, whether sharing their stories with the Everyday Sexism Project, raising issues at home or work, or boldly putting their heads above the parapet on social media. Those who suggest it is lazy or ineffectual to speak out online have clearly never experienced the barrage of abuse that this so often brings.

But among the hate and the harassment, nothing makes me smile like the stories from women and girls who are taking matters into their own hands. At one school I visited, girls had noticed on Twitter that the students at the local boys' school, who were due to join them for my talk, were resistant to the idea of a discussion about sexism, and planning to be as disruptive as possible. Determined to see a productive session go ahead, the girls left their lessons five minutes early and, arriving at the auditorium ahead of the boys, spaced themselves out so they were sitting in every other chair. Forced to sit interspersed between the girls and denied the dominant dynamic of a dissenting bloc, the protesters had the wind taken out of their sails and even found, to their surprise, that there was far less to object to than they had anticipated.

What's even more exciting is the ever-increasing number of

young people, including boys, who approach me after school talks to ask for advice in combatting sexism and setting up school societies to tackle the problem. Reports suggest that over 200 new feminist societies have been set up in the past few years alone at UK schools and universities, and ever more young people feel comfortable associating themselves with the label.

And for anyone who honestly still wants to argue that we no longer need feminism, I no longer spout endless statistics to try and convince them, I simply present them with these two quotes about women.

> 'It is the law of nature that woman should be held under the dominance of man.'
>
> CONFUCIUS, CIRCA 500 BC

> 'I think that putting a wife to work is a very dangerous thing ... When I come home and dinner's not ready, I go through the roof.'
>
> DONALD TRUMP (NOW PRESIDENT OF THE UNITED STATES), 1994

Clearly, we still have a long way to go.

SHARING STORIES OF SEXISM
ON SOCIAL MEDIA IS TWENTY-
FIRST-CENTURY ACTIVISM

Tweeting about sexism could improve women's well-being, according to a new study published in the *British Journal of Social Psychology*. The study suggests that a sense of 'collective action' may be at the root of the benefits. Participants were divided into groups: some were asked to tweet publicly, some privately and some not to tweet at all. According to the abstract, 'only public tweeters showed decreasing negative affect and increasing psychological well-being, suggesting tweeting about sexism may serve as a collective action that can enhance women's well-being'.

Since launching the Everyday Sexism Project in 2012, I've seen first-hand the positive impact that sharing stories via social media can have. I've seen women tweet their experiences of street harassment and receive support, understanding and solidarity from others all over the world. I've seen a woman tweet a story of workplace discrimination and receive a reply from an HR manager in a different city, offering to lend their expertise to help. I've received messages from men explaining that they've come across these tweets unexpectedly, and feel that their eyes have been opened to a problem they hadn't previously been aware of.

So the results of this study do not come as a surprise to me. But they may come as a surprise to those who argue that using social media to try to advance social justice amounts to lazy 'clicktivism' by futile 'keyboard warriors'.

It is often argued that the recent wave of online feminism is somehow lessened by its medium, or that sharing experiences online weakens victims, giving them an 'easy' way out instead of reporting incidents elsewhere. This line of thought fundamentally fails to recognize the very nature of gender inequality, which is often subtle, cumulative and deeply ingrained. Not every instance of everyday sexism is something that could be reported elsewhere, but having a forum to share these grievances can help victims to take back a sense of power and control – a sense of protest over powerlessness. Don't underestimate the catharsis and empowerment that can come simply from telling your story and having it accepted and believed, in a world where it is so often ignored or brushed off.

Those who argue that sharing these stories online prevents justice being done couldn't be more wrong; indeed, the opposite is true. We live in a world in which many victims of sexual violence or discrimination are made to feel guilty, or blamed for their ordeals, or simply do not believe they will be taken seriously. It is this that holds them back from reporting, not the fact that an online forum is available to share their experiences. The women who share their stories online aren't doing it instead of an official report they would otherwise have made; they are doing it to break what would previously have been silence.

Hundreds explicitly mention in their tweets or posts that they have never felt able to share their story with anyone before – even partners or family – let alone reporting it to the police. What's more, a great number of women have written in to Everyday Sexism to reveal that they have found the courage to report an assault to the police, or workplace harassment to their employer, precisely because the stories of other women online have given them the strength to realize they are not alone, and that they have the right to stand up.

One student told me that it was only after seeing a feminist video shared on Twitter that she realized what she had experienced could be classified as sexual assault. A runner wrote that when a man assaulted her in the street, it was the other women's stories she had read online that gave her the strength to stop, take down his car number plate and report him to the police. A teacher wrote that after she shared the stories with the girls in her class, they started their own feminist society and began to stand up to sexism at school. What happens online doesn't stay online. Its impact can be far wider.

Of course, social media isn't perfect – perhaps no single form of activism is. For a start, it excludes those without access to the internet or electronic devices, which is a major problem, so it needs to be used in conjunction with other efforts. In addition, social media users posting on topics such as sexism may face vitriolic abuse from trolls. But its capacity to spread an idea to millions of people around the world is undeniable and unique, as hashtags such as #YesAllWomen, #YouOKSis and #WhyIStayed have proved. And while activism shouldn't start and end with the internet, the point is that different methods can combine together to effect change. Social media can be one starting point from which wider efforts grow.

At Everyday Sexism, for example, we take many of the stories shared with us online and use them to create real change offline; using them to start conversations around consent and healthy relationships in schools, for example. That way, those who might not have accessed the project online are still included through outreach in the community. We use the thousands of entries we receive from women in the workplace to provide politicians and businesses with an idea of the kind of abuses women are still facing in their careers, from maternity discrimination to sexual assault. We used the stories we had received from women on public transport to inform our work with the British Transport Police on Project Guardian, which included the retraining of 2,000 members of staff around victim-centred principles, and has raised reporting of sexual offences on London transport by 35 per cent.

Writing a tweet isn't the same as going on a march, or writing to a member of parliament, but it is valuable in its own right. As we battle to shift deeply ingrained sexist norms, it matters that millions of people are able to stumble across the feminist message and see those norms challenged on social media. It is a new way to reach those who might not ever deliberately seek out the message elsewhere.

Just as it is frustrating to see feminists constantly told that they are fighting the 'wrong' battles, it is equally reductive to suggest they shouldn't be using the 'wrong' platforms. Why shouldn't twenty-first-century feminism make use of every tool at its disposal?

Originally published 6 February 2015

FEMINISM ISN'T DEAD, DESPITE ALL THE ASSASSINATION ATTEMPTS

Feminism is dead. Long live feminism. The front page of the *Spectator* and a spate of other articles would have us believe the battle is won and we can now 'move on'.

I can't be the only one who thinks this is wonderful news. We highly strung, hand-wringing, oversensitive, perpetually offended wilting violets can hang up our suffragette-coloured hats, stop combing Twitter in desperate search of minor criticism to weep about and finally stop hating all the men for long enough to get boyfriends. Rejoice!

Except . . . there are still just a few minor issues to sort out. As kind as it is of the *Spectator* (that great bastion of equality, which recently brought us a blow-by-blow comparison of the looks of the female Labour leadership contenders) to let us poor weary feminists off the hook, there's a bit of a catch. Women are still being murdered by their male partners every week; 85,000 of us are still being raped each year and 400,000 sexually assaulted; while 54,000 of us lose our jobs each year because of maternity discrimination. British women earn about 19 per cent less than men overall, there are fewer of us running FTSE 100 companies than there are men named John. We are the majority of low-paid workers and the domestic and caring work we do is unpaid and undervalued. At school, one-third of us will suffer unwanted sexual touching, also known as sexual assault, between the ages of sixteen and eighteen. One in four of us will experience domestic violence. But you already know all that. You've heard it all before. The *Spectator* and others are terribly thoughtful to offer us a break, because it is a bit tiring, really, to repeat these statistics over and over again. It's difficult to keep banging on about a problem that remains unsolved, while a vocal section of the population sticks its fingers in its ears and sings: 'Nah nah nah nah naaaah, I can't hear you!'

There is a bit of a glitch in their plan though, because angrily denying that a problem even exists tends to be one of the clearest indicators that a society has yet to get to grips with it.

So what is the source of this growing angst about feminism? If the movement truly were fading to an obscure death, as so many commentators suggest, you might think that front-page articles declaring its proponents 'feminazis' and trumpeting its demise would hardly be necessary. The real clue is to be found in the articles themselves, which fixate on objections to wolf whistles and urge us to get a grip and admit that the real reason for the under-representation of women in politics is women's own gooey fixation with babies. (Don't worry, there'll be an emergency feminist meeting where we can get together and work out what to do now the secret ovary-aching truth has been revealed.)

Both arguments suggest a stricken, defensive desire to deflect any sense of blame from the majority of men. If we maintain that there might be some connection between the treatment of women's bodies as public property in the street and the fact that they are discriminated against in the workplace, we're suddenly suggesting wolf-whistlers might have to reconsider their behaviour. If we foist the burden for discrimination on women's own uncontrollable hormones, there's no longer any public responsibility to do anything about the problem, because it's perfectly natural.

Some are also keen to remind us that we once had a female prime minister and the Queen is a woman, so what on earth can we still have to make a fuss about? And there's a feverish desperation to portray modern feminism as obsessed with body hair and lipstick, issues that weren't exactly top of the agenda when Sisters Uncut staged their protest at the *Suffragette* premiere, objecting to deep cuts to vital domestic violence services.

What's really happening here is an increasing anxiety among those in positions of power about the growing impact of feminism. So, there is a defensive attempt to undercut it by painting feminists as wailing whingers crying about nothing, or humourless harpies attacking innocent men. We saw this in the Sir Tim Hunt case, when the scientist gave a speech in which he advocated sex-segregated laboratories, saying: 'Let me tell you about my trouble with girls . . . three things happen when they are in the lab . . . You fall in love with them, they fall in love with you and when you criticise them, they cry.' As a result, UCL took the independent decision to discontinue his relationship with the university as an ambassador, an outcome subsequently portrayed as the brutal destruction of a noble, misunderstood man by an influential, furious online mob. But all this falls down a bit if you stop to take a quick look at the actual online feminist response, which focused largely on a humorous and positive campaign by female scientists to raise awareness of their diverse work.

So I hope you'll forgive me if I decide, on reflection, to forgo the first part and just stick with the second: long live feminism.

Originally published 25 October 2015

THE BEST COMEBACKS TO SEXIST COMMENTS

When you experience sexism or sexual harassment, it's common to feel a wave of emotions wash over you – fear, anger, embarrassment, shame, and often shock or panic. It's often incredibly difficult to respond in the heat of the moment, and victims frequently report the frustration of feeling frozen. Sometimes you think of a witty comeback hours later and wish you'd had it at the tip of your tongue in time.

Let's be very clear – it is never a victim's duty or responsibility to shout back. We won't solve any kind of sexism by telling the people experiencing it to react in a certain way; we'll only stop it by preventing the perpetrators from doing it in the first place. Often, it's not safe to respond, particularly if you are isolated, or fear the situation could escalate. But for those times when you do wish you had a quick comeback, the Twitter followers of the Everyday Sexism Project shared a deluge of wonderful, witty responses this week.

Some were delightfully cunning.

> @KariAnnSpriggs: when I get harassed I always pretend I didn't hear & say 'What?' The more they have to repeat the sillier they sound.

> @CannibalKisses: 'A woman's place is in the kitchen' you know what you're right. Lemme grab a knife.

@lolly_chops: guy makes orgasm noise at me
as I walk past. Me: 'That will probably be the
only time you ever hear that noise in your life.'

@KrezzyNL: a guy kept harassing me for my
phone number so I gave him the number
of another sexist, figured they'd have a lot
in common.

@butterworthamy: Someone bleeped at me from
a car as I was striding down the road. I yelled
'I AM A WOMAN NOT A TRAFFIC JAM.'

@_sallypreston_: Man: 'Nice tits.' Me: 'If you're
going to be a sexist pig at least be accurate. I
have fantastic breasts.' Silence . . .

Some favoured actions over words.

@NettyH: 5yo daughter got told by a 7yo boy
at the park that 'boys are best'. She promptly
out performed him on monkey bars.

Some whipped out their secret weapons.

@eleanorhydenl: two French men on Tube
discussing me in Fr: 'She's far too tall [6'+]
for a woman'. Me: *'Oui, elle parle français
en plus'*

@CleoR7: Managed to stop white van full of men mid-catcall by shoving a big powdery donut into my mouth then smiling with mouth full.

Others showcased wit and wordplay.

@Kathkinson: Bloke: 'You're a bit too thin for me'. Me: 'That's lucky because you're a bit too thick for me.'

@butterworthamy: MAN: 'Ive got the F, C and K, all I need is U' ME: 'I've got the B, Y and E, so I don't need U.'

@AineSays: Him: 'Look darlin, I don't mean to hassle you but . . .' Me: 'WELL THEN DON'T HASSLE ME.' . . .Then he got aggressive #charmer

@DemonicDragon: Guy on train after I asked him to move his bag off seat: 'Why don't you grab my cock?' Me: 'I didn't bring any tweezers.'

@Gareth_E_Slater: Dealing with a complaint, person didn't like amount I offered. 'I want to speak to your manager, and make sure it's not some woman', 'My boss is a woman', 'What about her boss' is the reply, 'She is too' I replied he stated 'I'll complain to the director if I have to'. 'Erm, not sure what she'd have to say'. He hung up!

@AlternateRowan: Male colleague: 'Don't mind her, she's on her period.' Me: 'If I had to bleed to find you annoying, I'd be anaemic.'

@_Vickycee: A friend heard a guy shout 'Sit on my face!' at a girl who replied 'Why, is your nose bigger than your dick?' AMAZING!

@Karen_M_Evans: New job, 1st meeting, only woman, suit asks where's the coffee? Reply Don't know, but when you find it mine's white no sugar.

And some really turned the tables.

@RachLittlewood: flashed at on a bus when I was 19. Snorted and said I'd seen more meat on a butcher's apron. Flasher got off bus head low.

@punk_manners: On train home guy rubs my bum. I grab hand, lift it in the air & say 'has anyone lost a hand? I found this one on my arse!'

@soapachu: 'cor look at the tits on that!' 'Yes, well at least one of us has something worth shouting about.'

@MistressLoz: Last time a man called me a bitch for ignoring his unwelcome advances, I barked at him loudly & repeatedly until he ran away.

Some came from awesome male allies.

> @tauriqmoosa: Ran up excitedly to car filled with
> dudes after they hooted at my friends. They
> sped away.

> Another recent fave from a man: 'Apparently
> the answer to "are you a legs man or a tits
> man" isn't "sorry I'm not a sexist"'

And others came from men who had experienced
sexism themselves.

> @philkemp1975: I'm 6'7 . . . drunk woman
> grabbed me and said 'Is "everything" in
> proportion?' I said 'Sadly not. If it was I would
> be 7'7.'

But my personal favourite was just sheer kick-ass comedy gold.

> @RosieBalls: A man once pointed out loudly that
> I have huge boobs. I looked down at them and
> screamed like I'd never noticed them before.

Originally published 6 December 2013

SHOUTING BACK: HOW WOMEN ARE FIGHTING STREET HARASSMENT

Nobody should be surprised at official statistics showing that one in five women over sixteen in England and Wales has been the victim of a sexual offence. Just before last week's report was launched and in response to a flurry of post-New Year accounts of harassment, the Everyday Sexism Project invited women to share their experiences of harassment on Twitter using the hashtag #ShoutingBack. Some 3,500 did so within the first five days.

The frequency of incidents reported is alarming: 'Every day since I was fourteen . . .' 'I've lost count of the number of times . . .' 'Called a bitch, whore, slut, slag on the street too many times to mention' were just a few of them. One woman said: 'On street, bent to tie my shoe, man walks pass, sticks hand inside my top, into my bra & squeezes breast.' Another described being 'force-kissed by a stranger in the street in broad daylight'. One woman, a cancer patient, told how a man openly elbowed his friend as she passed and said: 'You missed it. Totally bald. Proper dyke.'

Many incidents happened on public transport, from 'a man . . . putting his hand up my skirt and stroking my legs' on a packed Tube, to a woman who tried to get off the train only to have a man grab her breasts and tell her 'This isn't your stop, love'. Another victim said a man 'asked me to get off and f*** him . . . then tried to force my head into his lap'.

The theme of harassers becoming aggressive upon rejection was also repeated again and again. One woman said shouts of

'Hey ... come here' switched to 'You whore, I'll beat you so hard' when she refused. Another described being 'followed by a car of teenage boys who then tried to reverse into me when I wouldn't talk to them'. In one case, 'harassment started on the street, asking if I was married, ended with sexual assault on my doorstep at 3pm'.

Threats of violence and sexual assault, such as 'If I knew where you lived, I'd follow you home and rape you', were frequently reported, as were actual physical assaults. One woman was 'chased to my door at 11.30pm by two lads who "didn't want to hurt me". I ran faster.'

Nat Guest, a 26-year-old digital marketer from London, was walking home from a party on the morning of New Year's Day, when a man came up behind her, making 'sexual overtures'. When she didn't respond, he told her he had a knife and forced her to face a wall before masturbating into the back of her dress.

Although the police were supportive, the male officer said: 'Usually I'd tell you to avoid walking around on your own late at night, but, you know – New Year's. You have to get home somehow.' As a young woman in London, Guest experiences sexual harassment so frequently ('most days') that when she reflects on the incident, she says: 'Theoretically, I feel angry about it but emotionally I don't feel much at all apart from resigned. But the fact that I feel resigned to this type of thing makes me feel angry.'

Most worrying of all was the number of accounts that described the sexual harassment and assault of young girls. One said: 'While walking home last year, a man inside a parked car ask[ed] me for a blowjob. I was fifteen and in school uniform.' One recounted 'being told by my parents not to stand up for myself because that will get me raped'.

Holly Kearl, founder of the US-based organization Stop Street Harassment, says: 'Street harassment is often an invisible problem or one that is portrayed as a joke, compliment or the fault of the harassed person. In reality, it's a human rights violation.'

As one of the male supporters of #ShoutingBack tweeted: 'We have the power to stop street harassment. Don't do it. Don't let other men do it.'

Until they stop, we will keep shouting back.

Originally published 15 January 2013

DARTH VADER IS FOR GIRLS, TOO:
THE YOUNG FAN WHO FORCED
DISNEY TO CHANGE TOY LABELS

Star Wars fan Izzy Cornthwaite wanted a Darth Vader costume and lightsabre for her eighth birthday. But, upon exploring the UK Disney Store's website with her mum, Rebecca, she was devastated to see that the outfit was listed as a 'boy's costume'. 'Her face fell,' says Rebecca. Her eyes 'filled with tears and she said "I can't have it, it says they're only for boys."' But Izzy decided not to take it lying down and, following a quick chat with her mother about gender stereotypes, she wrote to Disney to explain her sadness about how the costume was labelled.

About a week later, she received a reply: 'The description for this costume has now been amended as we understand that all our little Jedis enjoy *Star Wars*.' Izzy went online to check for herself, and was delighted to find that it wasn't only the description of the Darth Vader costume that had been changed – the wording on everything from costumes to toys, Disney princess tutus to Hulk outfits was now labelled 'for kids', instead of being divided by gender.

Izzy is not alone in liking toys such as cars and fire engines, as well as dolls, from a very young age. Yet all stores clearly define their products by gender – 'If you visited a toy shop, you would actually see boys and girls going to their respectively gendered aisle,' says Rebecca. 'Some might argue, "What does this matter?"' But Rebecca believes the impact of this early delineation doesn't end in the toy aisle: 'We know that women are under-represented in many work roles and I feel very strongly that I don't want Izzy to avoid a career later in her life because it is a "boy's job", when I know she is capable of doing anything she sets her heart on.'

We can take hope from this and the string of other incidents where companies have listened to young people's concerns about gender stereotyping. Earlier this year, Clarks announced plans to bring out a wider range of unisex children's shoes after 8-year-old Sophie Trow wrote to complain that she wasn't allowed the dinosaur shoes she wanted as they were 'only for boys'. In a message shared by her mum on Twitter, Sophie wrote: 'Why can't girls have dinosaur shoes? I don't like how girls have flowery shoes. I like dinosaurs and fossils, so I think that other girls might as well.'

And last month, 8-year-old Els wrote to children's book publisher Scholastic to complain that it had labelled an exciting pirate book 'for boys'. After she started a petition and collected signatures from eighty friends and teachers at Bounds Green School, Scholastic agreed to end the gendered labelling of its books and removed gendered categories from its website. Els told *The Independent*: 'Girls may not like things that are labelled "for girls", they might want a monster book labelled "for boys". Books should be for everyone and we all like different things.'

It's a positive sign of what change might lie ahead, as more and more young people are speaking out against gender stereotypes – and companies are beginning to listen. These might sound like small victories, but together they are part of a real shift in the way big businesses are approaching the marketing of children's toys and clothes. This change has the capacity to have a major impact on young people's ideas about the world and their place in it. 'I want other children to be able to go into a shop and choose whichever toy they like,' says Izzy. 'I don't want them to feel embarrassed because they are a girl buying a "boy's toy" or a boy buying a "girl's toy". I like Lego and *Star Wars*, but I have to go to the boys' section to look at them. I think this should change.'

It's exciting to see a new generation of girls who already feel able, aged as young as eight, to stand up for themselves and declare their right to step outside the rigid pink and blue boundaries of gender stereotypes. May the force be with them.

Originally published 3 June 2015

SO FEMINISTS SHOULDN'T USE HUMOUR TO COUNTER SEXISM? YOU'RE HAVING A LAUGH

This week, a Twitter account called @talkSPORTdrive_ (not to be confused with the account of the popular radio show, @talkSPORTdrive) tweeted the following charming request:

> It's #TitsoutTuesday girls give me some
> entertainment before the game starts!!

Almost immediately, two obliging women responded. The first wrote: 'Here's a lovely pair' . . . but the picture of two pretty garden birds might not have been exactly what the folk behind the request had in mind. The second was equally forthcoming, offering up 'a nice pair of jugs' in beautiful ceramic shades.

After I retweeted the request to the Everyday Sexism Project's Twitter followers, more responses flooded in thick and fast. Over the course of the next forty minutes, those lucky chaps at the @talkSPORTdrive_ Twitter account received a veritable visual feast of all things tit-related. They saw some lovely (floured) baps . . .

A pair of (large-beaked) boobies . . .

A massive (dishwasher) rack . . .

A couple of shapely pairs of (table) legs . . .

A lovely (fur) muff . . .

Some big (weaponized) bazookas . . .

A couple of huge (sports) hooters . . .

And even a cute little ass (donkey) . . .

I could go on, but you get the picture. And would you believe it, within the hour the account that had issued the original request was mysteriously closed down. It was almost as if they didn't want to see any tits (or boobies, or knockers, or bazookas) after all.

No, of course it wasn't the most important feminist victory of all time, but it left me smiling. Quickly, however, I started receiving messages from people (mainly men) suggesting that to use humour as a means of communicating feminist ideas was to belittle the severity and importance of the cause. The tone of my response, it seemed, was not angry or serious enough for them. And this is a common charge levelled at feminists – that they are being TOO FUN and should put on a frown and get on with the proper business of being the shrieking harpies they've so often been painted as.

Every feminist should have the right to convey their message through whatever medium they choose, whether it be academic articles, performance art, short films or gut-wrenchingly funny jokes. I've never understood the stern Dworkin quote that has been adopted in so many social media bios: 'Feminist: not the fun kind'. Surely each method, from feminist literature to feminist stand-up, is likely to resonate with and engage a different audience (with some overlap, of course), and don't we need all the support we can get? What about reserving the right to be (justifiably) very angry one day, and use humour as a weapon the next?

The strongest argument in favour of feminist humour, though, is the enormous effect to which it can be used. Laughing at a problem doesn't just mean avoiding or belittling it – it can be one of the most powerful and effective ways to expose and tackle it. Since I started the Everyday Sexism Project, I've seen hundreds of women and men perfectly demonstrate humour's ability to debunk sexism. Here are a few of my favourites . . .

'Once had a guy ask: "Would you mind telling me your bra size?" I replied: "No, but tell me first how big your cock is!" Amazingly he was shocked and found MY comment highly inappropriate.'

'I was walking to college when a group of thirtysomething men approached me. One of them asked me: "Is it true you can get an orgasm from riding a bike?" (I wasn't even riding one.) I replied: "I'm more likely to get an orgasm from a bike than you." His friends all laughed at him as I walked away.'

'Guy at work used to think it was okay to only ever address me as "big boobs". "Morning, big boobs" etc. I started addressing him as "small penis" – he soon realized that maybe saying "Morning, Kate" would be a better way to address me.'

'Guy on bus: "Do you know where the Playboy club is?" Me: "Sure, it's the next stop." That 25-minute walk'll learn him. #haHA'

'Dear guy I caught jacking off in your car while staring at me on the sidewalk, please enjoy the giant dent in your door.'

Originally published 22 November 2013

WHAT I HAVE LEARNED FROM FIVE YEARS OF EVERYDAY SEXISM

In spring 2012, a week after setting up a website to catalogue experiences of gender inequality, I asked Lady Gaga for her support via Twitter. Keen to raise awareness of my newly created Everyday Sexism Project, I hoped she might spread the word among her millions of followers.

The next morning, I sleepily reached for my phone and saw more than 200 new notifications. I clicked eagerly on the first message and stopped cold. It wasn't, as I had hoped, the first of many new entries from women who had suffered harassment or assault. It was a brutally graphic rape threat – and the moment I became aware of the sheer force of hatred that greets women who speak out about sexism.

The threats continued to flood in. The sheer tenacity was startling. Who were these men, who could spend days, weeks – years, even – bombarding a woman they had never met with detailed descriptions of how they would torture her?

Over time, things became clearer. I met men who opposed feminism in different settings, and began to recognize their varied tactics. In some ways, the online abusers – who hurled hatred from behind a screen – were the least threatening. The repetition in their arguments (if you can call 'get off your high horse and change your tampon' an argument) made it clear that their fury was regurgitated: rooted in a fear of that man-hating, society-destroying 'feminazi' of online forum fantasy.

More sinister were the slick, intelligent naysayers who hid in plain sight. Men who scoffed at social events, confidently assuring those around us that sexism in the UK was a thing of the past and I should look to other countries to find 'real problems'. Men who asked my husband, in commiserating tones, how he coped with being married to me. Politicians who told me I was 'unnecessarily negative' and that girls these days didn't know how lucky they were. The newspaper picture editor who overlooked the content of my interview when he announced his priority was to make me look 'as sexy as possible'. People with the power to change things and the will to keep them exactly the same.

Despite this, the site was a success, and over the next five years, hundreds of thousands of testimonies flooded in. Almost every woman or girl I met told me their story, too. A 9-year-old who had received a 'dick pic'. An elderly lady who had been assaulted by her late husband's best friend. A young black woman refused entry to a nightclub while her white girlfriends were waved through. A woman in a wheelchair who was told she would be lucky to be raped. My assumptions about the type of person who suffers particular forms of abuse and the separation between different kinds of prejudice quickly shattered.

The sadness of the stories was a heavy thing to bear, as was the continued abuse I received. An interviewer asked me live on air whether it was difficult having no friends because I was so humourless. An American commentator wrote a blog publicly warning my husband he would one day come home to find I had burned down our house, murdered our children and joined a 'coven of lesbian witches'. Somewhere around the time I received a death threat alongside the claim I was a dripping poison that should be eradicated from the world, I started seeing a counsellor. And at times I seriously considered the coven.

But there were pleasant surprises, too. I hadn't anticipated the practical and emotional help offered by other women – solidarity from those of my own age and staunch support from older feminists who had seen it all before. And nothing could outweigh the privilege of being entrusted with so many people's stories, often never told before. I felt a great sense of responsibility to make sure women's voices were heard.

Another joy was being part of a burgeoning wave of feminism, standing alongside others tackling everything from media sexism to female genital mutilation. Perhaps the most important lesson I learned was how closely connected the different forms of inequality are. It is vital to resist those who mock and criticize us for tackling 'minor' manifestations of prejudice because these are the things that normalize and ingrain the treatment of women as second-class citizens, opening the door for everything else, from workplace discrimination to sexual violence.

To be a feminist, I have learned, is to be accused of oversensitivity, hysteria and crying wolf. But in the face of the abuse the project uncovered, the sheer strength, ingenuity and humour of women shone like a beacon. The dancer who performed for hours on the Tube to reclaim the space where she was assaulted. The woman who waited five years to present her contract and a salt cellar to the careers adviser who had told her he would eat her paperwork if she ever became an engineer. The pedestrian who calmly removed the ladder of a catcalling builder, leaving him stranded on a roof.

That's why I can honestly say that the experiences and

lessons of the past five years have left me more hopeful than despairing. I can't celebrate this milestone, exactly, representing as it does a collective outpouring of grief, anger and trauma. But I think of the resilience, the solidarity, the resistance, and I can't mourn it either. In five years, I have learned that the problem is immense, but the will to fight it is greater still.

Originally published 17 April 2017

Afterword

AFTERWORD

In 2014, UN special rapporteur on violence against women Rashida Manjoo described the UK as one of the most sexist countries she had recently visited. Describing a 'boys' club sexist culture', she said there was 'a more visible presence of sexist portrayals of women and girls' and a 'marketisation of women's and girls' bodies' in the UK, which was more pervasive than elsewhere. 'Have I seen this level of sexist cultures in other countries?' she asked: 'It hasn't been so in-your-face.'

If Manjoo's assessment succinctly summed up the UK's misogyny problem, our response only confirmed it. A male *Telegraph* writer dismissed her conclusions as 'pure nonsense'. Another male columnist wrote that she 'could hardly be more wrong'. Daytime radio and television programmes went into overdrive, scrambling indignantly to quote rape statistics from different countries around the world (ignoring the fact that Manjoo had not specifically referenced rape), as if they could magically erase the number of women assaulted and murdered in the UK on a weekly basis. One radio programme invited me on to discuss the statement, opening the interview by demanding that I confirm their belief that the UK was, in reality, far less sexist than other countries. Slowly, I replied that it was difficult for me to answer the question with scientific accuracy, given that my work had begun only relatively recently, and that my project was qualitative rather than quantitative. If only, I mused aloud, there was some expert we could ask instead: somebody, perhaps, with over three decades of international human rights experience, who had been charged by a body like the United Nations with the explicit job of visiting different countries to assess their treatment of women . . .

In the five years spanned by these columns, there have been some slow changes, both big and small. John Lewis has ended the gender segregation of its children's clothes. The UK government, after intense pressure from campaigners, finally voted to ratify the Istanbul Convention and to make sex and relationships education a compulsory part of school education. The Supreme Court made the landmark ruling that employment tribunal fees are unlawful and must be abolished.

Other battles drag on. Free childcare and flexible working remain inadequate to prevent women's careers from suffering negative repercussions after having children. New shared parental leave allowance doesn't go far enough to begin to level the caring playing field. Sexual violence services and refuges continue to battle and compete for meagre funds. The gender pay gap persists. Recommendations by the Women and Equalities Committee for schools to tackle sexual violence have been rejected en masse by the government, despite new figures showing a wave of rapes and sexual assaults reported in schools. Opinion polls repeatedly

reveal that a large percentage of the British public blame
victims of rape for their own assault. Survivors of sexual
violence remain detained in Yarl's Wood Immigration
Removal Centre despite having committed no crime. And,
as I write, the government has revealed plans to remove supported housing from the welfare budget, a move that charity
Woman's Aid says would force over a third of refuges to close
their doors for good.

Meanwhile, the failure to acknowledge our society's endemic
sexual violence or to recognize the connections between these
different human rights violations stubbornly persists.

On Friday 29 September 2017, police found a woman's
body, later identified as police officer Leanne McKie, in a lake
in Cheshire. Police described the case as an 'isolated incident'.
Underneath the story on the *Guardian* website, an algorithm
automatically listed 'related stories'. The highlighted headlines included:

'WOMAN'S BODY FOUND IN LAKE AT
UNIVERSITY OF EAST ANGLIA'

'WOMAN'S BODY FOUND ON NORFOLK BEACH'

'WOMAN'S BODY FOUND IN WEST SUSSEX WOODS'

'WOMAN'S BODY FOUND AFTER
CANTERBURY SUPERMARKET SHOOTING'

'WOMAN'S BODY FOUND IN SNOWDONIA'

'WOMAN'S BODY FOUND IN SUITCASE'

'WOMAN'S BODY FOUND ON ESTATE'

Isolated incident indeed.

Of course, the police intended to reassure the public that this wasn't the work of a serial killer, but this wording, intentionally or not, erases and obscures the reality of the national picture of ongoing violence against women.

We can tackle each of these events individually, working to catch individual perpetrators and achieve justice for individual victims. But until we as a society acknowledge the devastating and far-reaching impact of daily misogyny and sexualized violence, we will never stem the tide. No single example of sexism automatically gives rise to a specific incident of misogynistic violence, the picture is far more complex than that. But when you step back and join the dots between each of the different examples outlined in this book, it is very hard to deny that the bigger picture reveals systemic and widespread inequality which goes to the very heart of our society.

We could draw, if not a straight line, then a meandering, dotted one, between the childhood messaging that girls are bad at STEM subjects, the hopeless publicity campaigns that compound the problem, the dearth of women in engineering and science and the creation of medicines and crash test dummies that endanger women's very lives.

Between the largely male front-page bylines, the sexist portrayal of female politicians, the explosion in online abuse of political women and the dramatic under-representation of women in our government.

Between the deliberately titillating portrayal of sexual violence in the papers, the rampant victim-blaming in our society, the low rates of reporting by victims and the paucity of convictions for rape.

Between the ubiquity of online pornography, the failure of schools, universities and government to tackle sexual harassment in education, the lack of sex and relationships education and the shockingly high rates of sexual assault on campus.

Within such a context, the repeated rape, murder, harassment and abuse of women is not a coincidence, or a series of one-off occurrences, but an inevitable, deadly conclusion. Every week that we fail to see the pattern, to acknowledge the invisible problem, and to take meaningful action, two more women pay with their lives.

Acknowledgements

I am enormously grateful to Jane Martinson, without whom this book, these columns and quite possibly my entire journalistic career would not have existed at all. To Bim Adewunmi, Nosheen Iqbal, Malik Meer, Kira Cochrane, Leah Harper, Pamela Hutchinson and Suzie Worroll, who I have been lucky enough to work with as editors, colleagues and friends at *The Guardian*, and who have guided, supported and championed me. To Patrick Kingsley and Lauren Wolfe, who supported me at the very beginning of my career and answered all manner of stupid questions.

I would like to thank the article subjects and interviewees who have been so generous with their time and expertise and the schools, universities and organizations that have allowed me to gather research and experience. I am, as always, deeply indebted to the thousands of inspiring, strong, clever, funny women who have shared their Everyday Sexism experiences with the project website and Twitter account. A big thank you to the members of Women in Journalism, who provided inspiration, encouragement and community. And to the members of the coven, for solidarity and support.

I am also deeply indebted to my wonderful agent Georgia Garrett, to Madeleine Dunnigan and everybody at Rogers, Coleridge and White. And to Nicola Crossley, my fantastic, supportive and flexible editor, Jess Barrett, Melissa Bond, Claudia Connal, Amy Fulwood, Judith Long, Helen Upton and everybody at Simon & Schuster. It is always a joy to work with you all. Thanks also to my excellent and eagle-eyed copy-editor Jo Whitford for her tirelessly thorough and precise work, and to Pip Watkins for her gorgeous cover design.

Finally, to my family, friends and my husband, Nick, who provided staunch and stubborn support as these columns racked up some of the highest numbers of misogynistic, abusive and violent comments on the *Guardian* website. (It is tempting to remark with relief that there is no comments section in a published book, but try telling that to the men who responded to my first book by inserting handwritten notes in bookshops saying: 'Say no to feminism' and 'Women lie about rape'.) Thank you for keeping me going.